Technology with Intention

Dear Readers,

Much like the diet phenomenon Eat This, Not That, this series aims to replace some existing practices with approaches that are more effective—healthier, if you will—for our students. We hope to draw attention to practices that have little support in research or professional wisdom and offer alternatives that have greater support. Each text is collaboratively written by authors representing research and practice. Section 1 offers practitioner perspective(s) on a practice in need of replacing and helps us understand the challenges, temptations, and misunderstandings that have led us to this ineffective approach. Section 2 provides researcher perspective(s) on the lack of research to support the ineffective practice(s), and reviews research supporting better approaches. In Section 3, the author(s) representing practitioner perspective(s) give detailed descriptions of how to implement these better practices. By the end of each book, you will understand both what not to do, and what to do, to improve student learning.

It takes courage to question one's own practice—to shift away from what you may have seen throughout your years in education and toward something new that you may have seen few, if any, colleagues use. We applaud you for demonstrating that courage and wish you the very best in your journey from this to that.

Best wishes,
— *M. Colleen Cruz* and *Nell K. Duke, Series Editors*

Technology with Intention: Designing Meaningful Literacy and Technology Integration

SUZANNE KELLY AND ELIZABETH DOBLER

HEINEMANN
PORTSMOUTH, NH

Heinemann
145 Maplewood Avenue, Suite 300
Portsmouth, NH 03801
www.heinemann.com

Offices and agents throughout the world

The authors and publisher wish to thank those who have generously given permission to reprint borrowed material:

"Internet/Broadband Fact Sheet" from Pew Research Center, Washington, D.C., posted June 12, 2019: https://www.pewresearch.org/internet/fact-sheet/internet-broadband/. Used with permission of the publisher.

Excerpts from Common Core State Standards © Copyright 2010. National Governors Association Center for Best Practices and Council of Chief State School Officers. All rights reserved.

Credits continue on page vi

Library of Congress Cataloging-in-Publication Data

Names: Kelly, Suzanne, 1985– author. | Dobler, Elizabeth, 1963– author.
Title: Technology with intention : designing meaningful literacy and technology integration / Suzanne Kelly and Elizabeth Dobler.
Description: Portsmouth, NH : Heinemann Publishing, [2021] | Includes bibliographical references.
Identifiers: LCCN 2020055672 | ISBN 9780325118659
Subjects: LCSH: Computers and literacy. | Language arts—Computer-assisted instruction. | Educational technology. | Effective teaching. | Intentionality (Philosophy).
Classification: LCC LC149.5 .K45 2021 | DDC 371.33/4—dc23
LC record available at https://lccn.loc.gov/2020055672

Series Editors: Nell K. Duke and M. Colleen Cruz
Acquisitions Editor: Margaret LaRaia
Production Editor: Patty Adams
Cover Illustrator: James Yang
Cover and Interior Designer: Monica Ann Cohen
Typesetter: Valerie Levy, Drawing Board Studios
Manufacturing: Val Cooper

Printed in the United States of America on acid-free paper

1 2 3 4 5 MPP 25 24 23 22 21
March 2021 Printing

Dedication

This book is dedicated to all of my amazing colleagues and students who have been navigating this fun and sometimes frightening tech journey with me! It is also dedicated to my extraordinary mentor, principal Elizabeth Culkin, who has taught me the value of "believing and achieving it!" And finally, to my mother, who always supports and uplifts me throughout all of my life's endeavors.

—S.K.

To my family, thank you for supporting my technology learning, even if you remind me I can just Google that myself.

To those who have learned to become teachers and those who have worked to become better teachers during a pandemic. Hold on to your dream.

—E.D.

Credits continued from page iv

CONTENTS

INTRODUCTION

Nell K. Duke

As educators, I imagine that many of you have been to professional conferences with an exhibit hall: booth after booth of vendors selling programs, books, software, manipulatives, posters, papers and pencils, whiteboards, T-shirts, and on and on. Now imagine yourself at the equivalent exhibit hall for a medical conference. There, too, are books, software, all kinds of equipment—from syringes to massive imaging machines, posters, waiting room furniture, and yes, T-shirts.

When we think of the context of medicine, it is easy to grasp several truisms. First, none of these products can replace physicians. A deeply knowledgeable and skilled human is still necessary to the practice of medicine. Second, many of these products can help physicians do their job better. Physicians with access to a more rapid strep test and a more precise functional magnetic resonance imaging (fMRI) machine are likely to be more efficient and effective in their work. Third, physicians bring their expertise to bear in selecting and deploying these tools. For example, a great surgeon knows that this scalpel works very well cutting through skin in this part of the body but not as well in cutting through skin in this other part of the body; a great primary care physician concludes that this diet management app is likely to work for patients with one kind of health profile but not for patients with a different profile, and so on.

Now let's turn back to education and in particular education technology. Although perhaps less obvious to some, the same three truisms apply:

- Educational technology cannot replace a knowledgeable and skilled teacher.
- Educational technology can help teachers do their job better.

- Skilled teachers bring their expertise to bear in selecting and deploying educational technology.

This book helps us to live out these truisms, particularly with respect to literacy education. The title really nails it—technology *with intention.*

We solicited this book well before the COVID-19 pandemic. Even before the pandemic, conference exhibit halls, our email in boxes, and the web were overflowing with technological tools, some very promising, some decidedly not promising, and all underscoring the need for the expertise of educators to select among and deploy them in the service of children's learning. As we move toward a post-COVID-19 world, there are even more tools, with more on the way, and still the need for the expertise of educators to select and deploy them in the service of children's learning. Our goal is for this book to help you further develop and activate that expertise.

When I think about someone who knows research on literacy and technology *and* is able to provide highly practical, actionable advice for teachers, Elizabeth Dobler immediately comes to mind. I have known Beth a long time, and one of the qualities I most admire in her is that she has remained so well grounded in K–12 classroom practice even after many years in higher education. She is up on the latest technology tools and the day-to-day challenges and opportunities that classroom teachers face.

Suzanne Kelly is much newer to me. But *wow*. She has a vast knowledge of educational tech tools, but she does not let those tools distract her from knowing her students and focusing on effective instruction. She enacts daily the truism I offered earlier—"Skilled teachers bring their expertise to bear in selecting and deploying educational technology"—and she takes us along with her in that enactment. I think you'll find uses of technology she describes to be innovative and yet also reassuring—because they connect to existing understandings about how children learn and how effective teachers teach.

I am grateful to these authors for guiding us through the exhibit hall of today's technology for literacy, and I am grateful to you for your willingness to walk through that hall with them to provide the best education possible for children.

SECTION 1

NOT THIS

Technology Dictating Literacy Instruction

ELIZABETH DOBLER AND SUZANNE KELLY

If we were able to travel back in time to study the integration of digital technology into literacy instruction, even just a few years ago, what we would see would vary widely from state to state, school to school, even classroom to classroom. If states, districts, or schools saw value and had the means to use technology as part of literacy instruction, resources were directed toward supporting it. If they lacked the means, or did not prioritize it, technology was largely absent, apart from an occasional computer lab or laptop cart and perhaps one or two finished writing pieces a year that would be typed up and printed out. Technology instruction at the elementary level was seen by many as a local or personal preference, as well as often connected to the economic resources or lack thereof for the schools involved. In many, many places whether a teacher integrated technology into their classroom started not by considering its value, but whether it was even available. If it was available, the thinking then shifted to what it could be used for. There was a fair amount of controversy as to even whether technology was appropriate in the elementary school setting, so one of the questions a teacher would ask before diving into a unit that could involve technology was, *Should I use it?*

During the start of the COVID-19 pandemic, this dynamic suddenly shifted. Many of us found ourselves suddenly required to teach using technology out of pure necessity as entire states quarantined. States, districts, and school communities moved heaven and Earth to make sure as many students as possible had access to digital devices. The question no longer was, *Should I use technology?* or *What can I use this technology for?* but instead *How do I use technology to help meet the needs of the most students right now?* Some students had internet access; some did not. Some students had high-functioning hardware that allowed them to move in and out of various apps and platforms easily;

some did not. Many teachers saw participation in academics decrease as, without strong classroom community and teacher relationships, students had less of a reason to engage with learning.

We know most educators did the best they could with the resources they had at the time. It was an emergency, and triage was the required mode. We saw many teachers grow from novice to adept tech users over a period of weeks and others who found no- to low-tech ways of gathering student work, providing feedback, and maintaining community. We watched teachers conduct video conferences with student readers and writers, and sometimes a car or McDonald's parking lot was that teacher's conferring space because the teacher didn't have reliable internet or a quiet place to work. The open discussion nature of platforms like Zoom led some teachers to surrender the "mic" to students and guest speakers and move toward collaboratively created classroom time. We learned of teachers who became pen pals with their students, sending messages back and forth via text, email, and mailed letters. In rural areas with little internet access, some teachers logged impressive car mileage as they personally delivered learning packets and books to students' homes. Baltimore City Public Schools had their local cable station run teachers' video lessons throughout the day. Other teachers lobbied authors for digital access to texts for their students. So many teachers were able to stay connected to their students and offer engaging academics that helped their students grow even in the worst of times.

Now, with a little time under our belts, we pause to reflect on what can be learned, both by successes and mistakes. What were the challenges with technology and decision-making around technology that got in our way of doing the work students needed most? We want to make sure that the increased familiarity we have with tech due to COVID-19 is accompanied by true intentionality and strong pedagogy. Just because so many more teachers now know how to use a variety of tech tools doesn't mean that technology should always be our choice. As much now as ever, we need to center our decision-making around research-proven principles and practices. Will using technology

Just because so many more teachers now know how to use a variety of tech tools doesn't mean that technology should always be our choice.

in this instance make student learning more efficient, accessible, or authentic or less so? It can be very hard to make these decisions for our students when so many other people believe they have the right answer and that the answer is some specific piece of technology. Every one of us needs to be aware of the most common existing technology for the grade levels we teach and should be teaching students how to use and evaluate existing technology in appropriate ways. The decision of when and how to use the technology requires the thinking of the user. In other words, the primary question lying before us is, Which tech tools will help us meet the specific educational goals at hand—how do we use tech with intention?

Every one of us needs to be aware of the most common existing technology for the grade levels we teach and should be teaching students how to use and evaluate existing technology in appropriate ways. The decision of when and how to use the technology requires the thinking of the user.

What Technology Is (and Isn't Yet)

Technology is a tool. Any tool requires knowledge on the part of the user. Any tool can be misused. From *Metropolis* to *Westworld*, we communicate our chronic anxiety about technology outsmarting and overpowering humanity that surrender might be our best option. When we surrender to technology, we give up the opportunity to weigh options and choose the best course of action ourselves. Without that surrender being a conscious decision, fully informed by the specific context of the technology's use, we become more distant from the real work we should be doing.

Technology can take over some but not all of our decision-making. It can mean that we make some decisions less often than others: having a closetful of the same professional outfit worked for Barack Obama and Steve Jobs because it eliminated the daily decision of what to wear, but neither of them chose that one repeated outfit at random nor did they always wear that outfit regardless of changed circumstances. Steve Jobs didn't wear his black turtleneck in the heat of summer and

For decision-making guidelines on when to use technology, see Section 3, page 53.

Barack Obama doesn't wear his suit on family vacations. The decision-making they gave up was only the part that didn't need to be repeated. Jobs and Obama were avoiding decision fatigue, the unnecessary use of energy making choices that depletes our attention from the most important work we have to do. Because teachers face so much decision fatigue, technology can be an appealing outsourcing of some decision-making. That can be a very smart decision provided (1) the technology is right for our specific students' precise needs, and (2) the technology is giving us space to do higher-level work directly with students. We use an app/program for publishing (PowerPoint, Adobe Voice, Word) or gathering readings (Padlet, Google Docs) because it consolidates our decision-making for a specific purpose (or is more open to allow for multiple purposes). If students can choose the form of publishing, they might start in Word to gather their thinking. If they know they'll need to present the information in a visual format, then a digital slide app such as Google Slides might be the best choice. Yet often the purpose of our teaching doesn't guide our tech choices. It is not unusual to overhear teachers in the staff lounge mentioning the Google Slide project their kids are doing and then hearing the response being something along the lines of, "Oh, we're using Book Creator," with nary a discussion about how those tools will match or strengthen the literacy skills being taught. The focus is often on the tech tool itself, not the literacy skills prioritized. Teachers are inundated by a chorus of expectations: digital literacy, twenty-first century skills, college and career readiness, apps they *have* to know. It can be very difficult to sort out which voices we should listen to. Let's take a moment to name two of the messages teachers hear that argue we should surrender our decisionmaking to technology: "the future of work is technology" and "technology can avoid human error."

"The Future of Work Is Technology"

Education technology is a profitable and growing business. The education technology market for 2019 was $43 billion, growing from $39.33 billion in 2018 (Bridge n.d.). Ed tech companies have developed an effective narrative selling schools and districts on buying technology as the solution to their students' learning needs. The argument: to be competitive in the future professional marketplace, today's students need to be adept with technology. In addition, whole-district purchases of ed tech often originate from a panicked sense of scarcity: our students aren't performing well enough on standardized tests/these skills, and we need to fix this right away! We 100 percent agree that there is an urgency to improving students' learning now. Postponement is not the answer. However, outsourcing solutions to software programs without developing teacher expertise rarely yields more than a slight increase in student performance, as you'll see in Section 2. Additionally, although technology is indeed important, there is a danger in putting more stock in what the sales representative tells us are the skills and knowledge our students need, which just happen to align with what they're selling, as opposed to our trusting knowledge as professional educators.

We 100 percent agree that there is an urgency to improving students' learning now. Postponement is not the answer. However, outsourcing solutions to software programs without developing teacher expertise rarely yields more than a slight increase in student performance.

"Technology Leads to Efficiency"

When technology first entered the classroom, some feared computers would replace teachers. From addressing teacher shortages to saving costs, it is no coincidence that this solution most often occurs or is proposed in financially under-resourced districts. Still, without there being any evidence that tech can entirely replace teachers, people continue to argue for the efficiency of doing so. Of course, human beings will make errors, but, as of right now, they can respond to their own errors in ways that a computer program cannot. Teachers can see that their instruction isn't reaching a student and adapt. Computer programs can identify when but not why a student keeps picking the wrong answer. The program cannot discuss the task, determine the student's emotions and give support so that the student can produce their best work.

Yet, technology does allow for skills practice in a sequential, progressively difficult way. Often this can work when students need repeated and scaffolded practice of a concept, skill, or strategy on an individualized level. However, outsourcing that decision-making to technology so far has mostly meant that students practice skills in oversimplified, decontextualized tasks that often reveal only whether the student can complete that task, not the larger understanding behind the skill. Right now, much of ed tech software creates artificial contexts for students' learning that don't develop their understanding in meaningful, useful ways.

For the research on effective literacy learning with tech, see Section 2, pages 18–31.

Understanding Discomfort with Technology

Of course, sometimes the problem with technology isn't any outside source. It's us. Sometimes we are so overwhelmed with everything we have to do that we succumb to pressure from colleagues or supervisors to keep up with technology, drawing on what others are doing rather than making decisions on our own. Without an informed sense of purpose, even the best tech will be poorly used.

Teachers often aren't taught how to plan for tech fails, and so those failures can really derail instruction and alienate teachers from tech.

In fairness, too, technology can be unreliable. Every teacher we know has planned time for technology and then encountered tech performance issues that have meant lost learning time. How many of us have accessed devices for independent writing or research, only to have the wireless connection be spotty or the computers perform poorly because they are too outdated? Teachers often aren't taught how to plan for tech fails, and so those failures can really derail instruction and alienate teachers from tech.

Acknowledging the Digital Divide

Many schools make assumptions about students' access to technology at home, which further disadvantages some students. In some schools we boast that we offer internet access and devices for every student, but when schools have a device for every student, sometimes those devices aren't sufficiently up-to-date and internet performance can vary. During COVID-19, I (Suzanne) noticed that one of my high-performing students was not producing his usual quality of work. I asked him what I could do to help and learned that he had a very old device that often lagged. As a result, he became easily frustrated when attempting tasks and had adopted the attitude of completion with little care for the quality of his work. Once I identified the problem, I was able to help his family apply for a new device through New York City's Department of Education. While he waited for the device, I scheduled video chat check-ins with this student so he could tell me about his work and we could keep him on track. But it's important to note that I might not have inquired into this if there hadn't been such a change in his performance. That realization has made inquiry into students' work process with technology a regular element of my teaching.

We need to be very aware how much access to monetary resources can improve a student's learning experience in the digital world, and make sure we are making choices that don't create a gulf—commonly referred to as "the digital divide"—between our students with better access to tech and those who don't have the same resources. Additionally, many schools are drawn to programs and apps that are free or low cost when resources are tight, exchanging quality, privacy, exposure to advertisement, or proprietary agreements for free or inexpensive options. This means that often students who are the most vulnerable receive the lowest-quality and least protective digital learning options. Although the gap has decreased over time, it still exists.

You'll read more about the statistics on this in Section 2, with practical solutions in Section 3, pages 47–52.

How Are You Currently Using Technology to Teach?

I (Beth) vividly remember the moment I was asked this question and learned that technology wasn't meant for every single lesson but rather to enhance some lessons in a purposeful way. I very proudly raised my hand and said, "We are researching so my kids spend about twenty minutes of their reading block researching and recording data from the internet." The coach facilitating our group discussion asked, "Have you taught them how to 'read' on the internet? The transference of reading skills and strategies from a book to a device requires specific scaffolding for the context of digital reading." I was using technology as a tool but not giving students the necessary instruction—a common mistake for many of us. At the time, I felt totally deflated by the coach's question, but it was only by articulating what I was already doing that what I needed to do was revealed.

I was using technology as a tool but not giving students the necessary instruction—a common mistake for many of us.

Using technology for teaching and learning is not an all-or-nothing venture. In fact, we would guess that most teachers describe their technology use in the classroom as somewhere between very little and multiple times each day. The point isn't how much you use technology, it's what you and your students *do* with the technology. If you are recording data about the class pet onto a shared document, can the students make these entries? If three students are working on one device to research a topic, but only one student is doing the online searching, can you teach students how to collaborate using these skills? When students are assigned to create a digital project, have you taught how to use the tool before it's time to apply their new knowledge?

Take some time to reflect on how you currently use technology to teach. There is no judgment here. Technology use is what it is and will be what it can be with your effort to learn and grow. As you move on to the next section, you'll learn how much you already know about effective use of tech based on your knowledge of good literacy learning, and you'll deepen that knowledge with specific research about how tech can be used as a tool to support effective literacy learning.

SECTION **2**

WHY NOT?

What Works? Technology That Supports Active Literacy Learning

ELIZABETH DOBLER

As Suzanne and I explained in Section 1, the COVID-19 pandemic has meant that more educators use technology and are aware of students' inequal access to technology. We're grateful to be talking to increasing numbers of literacy educators about the potential of technology and the need for greater equity. To further that conversation, we're offering this synthesis of what the research tells us about the use of technology in literacy instruction so far. Of course, we know that every day new advances are emerging—artificial intelligence is working toward the goal of true differentiated instruction in response to an individual learner's experience; virtual reality is increasing our opportunities for experiential learning. Even with some of the unknowns presented by new technology, we have a strong basis for making informed decisions. Foundational understandings about effective literacy instruction and the use of technology in specific contexts help us use technology in intentional and informed ways. First, let's identify what research tells us gets in the way of effective use of technology in literacy learning.

Inequal Access

The statistics on access to technology tell the story of a divided learning experience. As of 2019, twenty-one million Americans lacked broadband access—the kind of high-speed reliable internet access needed to successfully use digital tools such as Zoom or video streaming when multiple users are in a close area—and schools have some of the highest rates of limited or no broadband access (Federal Communication Commission 2019). At home, students may not have access to a device or to broadband, or if they do have access, the device and/or broadband

In Section 3, pages 47–52, we will offer some ways of identifying and solving issues of access.

> *Perhaps eventually broadband access will be universal across the United States and the same level of working devices will be available to every student, but for now the digital divide is an unpleasant reality that teachers must figure out in their individual contexts.*

may be unreliable. Approximately 6 percent of Americans did not have access to the internet, but that figure is at 25 percent for those who live in rural areas (Federal Communication Commission 2019). To really get a clear picture of access, we also must consider affordability of broadband and the income gap between those who do and do not use the internet at home (see Figure 2–1).

Policy makers have issued or have tried to issue legislation to address the divide, but the work is ongoing and imperfect. Perhaps eventually broadband access will be universal across the United States and the same level of working devices will be available to every student, but for now the digital divide is an unpleasant reality that teachers must figure out in their individual contexts. The essential point is that we can't create a curriculum that assumes all students have equal access.

FIGURE 2–1 *Percent of Home Broadband Users by Income (Pew Research Center 2019)*

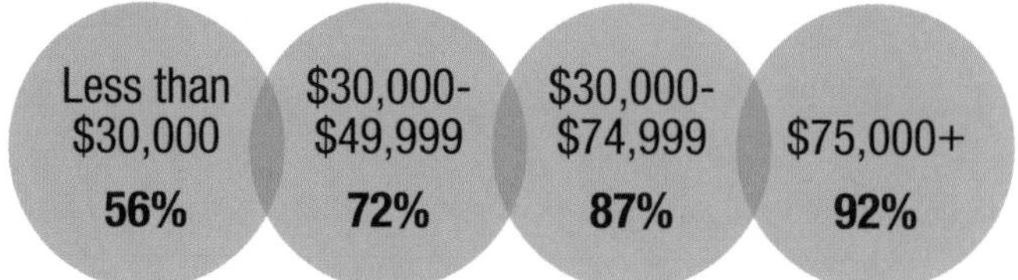

Understanding Technology and Effective Literacy Teaching

Of course, simply putting devices in to the hands of students is not enough. As devices and software change, our understanding of effective technology integration must continually evolve to meet the learning needs of our students. And yet, "new technologies are often applied to classrooms without an in-depth examination of their impact on learning before implementation" (F.-Y. Yang et al. 2018, 28). Because teachers have been left to figure

FIGURE 2–2 *Obstacles to Technology Integration for Teachers*

Obstacles to Technology Integration for Teachers
little value of tech as a teaching tool
limited tech knowledge and experiences
limited time to plan for meaningful tech use
reluctance to change teaching methods
overreliance on tech for skills practice

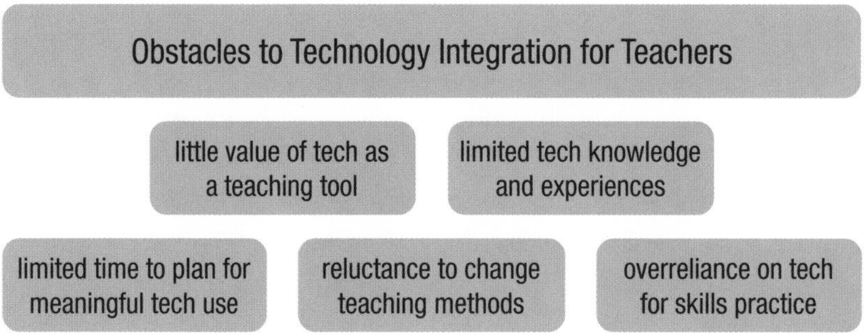

this out mostly on their own, research shows predictable patterns of struggle with effective tech integration (see Figure 2–2).

As adults, today's students will enter a global, knowledge-based economy, and many will work at jobs that do not yet exist. Yet traditional views of school and learning—the industrial-era school models that emphasize memorization, true-or-false and multiple-choice testing, and desks in rows—still exist in many schools. These traditionals view may keep some teachers from letting students realize the full potential of technology integration despite considerable empirical evidence of the efficacy of certain forms of tech (e.g., Little et al. 2018; Morphy and Graham 2012; Wouters et al. 2013). For students to demonstrate deeper learning and show mastery, they need to apply knowledge and skills through inquiry-based, project-based, and problem-based activities and authentic performances (Chen and Yang 2019; Furtak et al. 2012).

Effective integration of technology hinges on a teacher's understanding of how children learn and effective teaching practices, with and without technology.

Another obstacle may be the technology itself. Educational software can assess a student's reading skills, give instruction and practice at the student's level, and then assess again to determine progress. But software can't build a relationship with a child; it can't look into a child's face and recognize understanding or confusion. Education has a reputation for being quick to try new ideas, and unfortunately, research often lags behind classroom practice and does not always give us a clear-cut answer about technology's effectiveness in the classroom. Although research doesn't unequivocally tell us how to integrate technology, one idea is crystal clear. The successful integration of technology depends on a teacher's understanding of how children learn and effective teaching practices, with and without technology.

The key to moving beyond obstacles is to be aware of your own knowledge strengths and areas for growth and to recognize how these influence your instruction. Our knowledge of content, pedagogy, and technology all influence how we integrate technology into our teaching (Mishra and Koehler 2006). For example, you may be confident in your own knowledge of phonics (content) but ask students to complete a phonics worksheet in pdf form (technology). Although this activity utilizes technology, a more effective activity would be more interactive (e.g., movable digital letter tiles) and possibly use varied media (e.g., video, digital game) (pedagogy).

If you notice an area of your knowledge that needs a boost, whether it's content, technology, or pedagogy, seek out resources. Even as an educator with over thirty years of experience, over the past year I have found value in attending professional development for teaching reading (content), making digital resources accessible (technology), and developing individual accountability within group projects (pedagogy). As teachers we must continually learn! When you embrace this idea, your teaching will become better and you'll find more professional satisfaction. Let's explore what that looks like for literacy learning with technology.

Digital Literacy Is a Teaching Expectation

What's most essential for teachers' understanding is that technology plays an increasingly larger role in the ways we find and use information. It's not a question of *if* we use technology to teach reading and writing, but *how* we use technology to create the foundation for children to become literate adults. To function in today's world, students must learn print-based and digital literacy skills simultaneously. Nimbly moving from print to digital and back is a must for reading textbooks, library resources, news, and novels because these can be read on paper, an e-reader, a cell phone, or a computer.

Links within the texts can lead to websites, videos, and/or podcasts, requiring the reader to determine quality of the sources and to comprehend information in different formats. However, many teachers are in the difficult transition period of figuring out what digital literacy should look like. Some general expectations for literacy instruction and technology help get us started:

It's not a question of if *we use technology to teach reading and writing, but* how *we use technology to create the foundation for children to become literate adults. To function in today's world, students must learn print-based and digital literacy skills simultaneously.*

- The International Literacy Association calls for literacy instruction that prepares students to "produce, communicate, interpret, and socialize with peers" (2018, 2) in both digital and nondigital ways.
- The Common Core English Language Arts Standards (National Governors Association and Council of Chief State School Officers 2010) present expectations for integrating digital technologies into literacy instruction, promoting the notion that being literate and being digitally literate are synonymous (Dalton 2012) and calling on students to
  - integrate and evaluate content presented in diverse media and formats, including visually and quantitatively, as well as in words
  - use technology, including the internet, to produce and publish writing and to interact and collaborate with others
  - gather relevant information from multiple print and digital sources, assess the credibility and accuracy of each source, and integrate the information while avoiding plagiarism.

Although the standards do not specify how digital literacy skills should be taught, these expectations form a foundation for English language arts instruction in K–12 schools that necessitates technology being an integral part of the curriculum, not just an add-on. Technology should help students learn in ways not otherwise achieved—faster, more easily, with more depth. If technology merely replicates the ways we already learn, then it becomes a very expensive substitute for paper, pencil, and flash cards.

Technology should help students learn in ways not otherwise achieved—faster, more easily, with more depth. If technology merely replicates the ways we already learn, then it becomes a very expensive substitute for paper, pencil, and flash cards.

Becoming adept at the process of gathering information about ourselves and the world around us and communicating it with others are at the heart of literacy learning. If we think about this process, as adults, it's easy to see the ways technology makes literacy possible for us on a daily, hourly, and even moment-by-moment basis. Developing literacy skills needs to include technology to prepare our students for the traditional and digital literacy experiences they encounter each day.

Inquiry-Based Learning with Technology

To see the full benefits of technology in education, there must be a shift in pedagogy toward students being more active learners. Value must be placed on curiosity about the world, which leads to questions that drive active exploration of information. Asking questions, analyzing information, creating projects, and reflecting on learning are not just abstract values—they are consistently promoted in academic standards across various educational disciplines (see Figure 2–3).

FIGURE 2–3 *Standards Promoting Inquiry*

- Common Core State Standards for English Language Arts and Literacy
- Next Generation Science Standards
- College, Career, and Civic Life (C3) Framework for Social Studies State Standards
- Standards Framework for Learners (American Association of School Librarians)
- International Society for Technology in Education Standards for Students and for Educators

Inquiry learning supported with technology can enhance learning and provide students access to experiences that may not be available due to lack of funds, classroom time constraints, or the need for remote learning (Lakala, Lallimo, and Hakkarainen 2005) (see Figure 2–4 for benefits of integrating technology into inquiry). For example, viewing a time-lapse video of a plant's growth from a seed gives learners an additional or an alternative experience to growing plants in the classroom, leading to deeper understanding of plant life. Having students visit a World War II European battleground through Google Maps can spark new questions leading to such explorations as an interactive timeline of the battle. Research suggests integrating technology into inquiry learning can lead to higher achievement than using only a traditional method of teaching (e.g., textbook or teacher-directed) (Chang, Quintana, and Krajcik 2010; Hwang et al. 2013). Inquiry-based teaching using technology makes learning relevant, encourages metacognitive reflection and teamwork, and fosters creativity and collaboration (Saavedra and Opfer 2012). Intentional integration is the key. The use of technology enhances, not replaces, quality inquiry teaching and learning. See Figure 2–5 for ways integrating technology into inquiry learning benefits students.

FIGURE 2–4 *Positive Effects for Students from Inquiry Learning with Technology*

- Asking more and deeper questions (Buckner and Kim 2014)
- Using interactive models and simulations to experience a concept (Chang, Quintana, and Krajcik 2010; Colella 2000)
- Collecting and analyzing data to answer a question (McDonald and Songer 2008)
- Collaborating to solve problems (Barab et al. 2001)
- Creating products to share with others, and participating in learning communities near and far (Furtak et al. 2012)

FIGURE 2–5 *How Students Use Technology to Accomplish the Goals of Inquiry*

KEY ELEMENTS OF PROJECT-BASED LEARNING	INSTRUCTIONAL ACTIVITIES
Focus on thinking—design instructional activities to promote analysis, critical thinking, and depth of learning	▶ Gathering information (e.g., Kiddle search engine for kids, Newsela.org informational text) ▶ Evaluating information (e.g., Common Sense Media resources and lessons) ▶ Understanding information (e.g., digital books and websites, screen reader software, audio books, videos) ▶ Analyzing information (e.g., mind mapping and graphic organizer sites and apps) ▶ Creating projects to demonstrate new learning (e.g., Microsoft Sway, Adobe Voice)
Strive for authenticity—look for opportunities to bring real-world learning into the classroom and classroom learning into the real world	Creating digital video, audio recordings, and photos ▶ Hands-on learning activities (e.g., class garden, recycled materials construction project) ▶ Community issues (e.g., trash on a playground) ▶ Experts within the in-person and digital community (e.g., scientist, author, engineer)
Share projects—make students' projects available to others	▶ Sharing projects through digital communities (e.g., video conferencing presentation, Seesaw journal post) ▶ Using digital tools to discuss and give feedback (e.g., video conferencing breakout rooms or chat, Flipgrid)

KEY ELEMENTS OF PROJECT-BASED LEARNING	INSTRUCTIONAL ACTIVITIES
Work together—build students' capacity to collaborate with peers and adults	▶ Creating projects together using document sharing tools (e.g., Google Docs) and synchronous screen sharing tools (e.g., Zoom, Google Meet) ▶ Meeting with experts to learn more (e.g. children's authors, scientists, city officials)
Organize the work—teach students to organize their resources and work throughout the project	▶ Designing a work plan using a digital calendar, desktop sticky notes, graphic organizer sites, and apps (e.g., iThoughts, RWT Timeline)

(HQPBL 2018. www.hqpbl.org)

Inquiry activities may fall along a continuum from more to less teacher support: modeled, structured, guided, or open inquiry (Alberta Learning 2004). Factors influencing the amount of support include the students' experience learning with inquiry and learning with technology. Ultimately, we want students to create their own questions, search for answers, evaluate the quality of information, share new learnings, and use this knowledge to impact their community, because these are the skills needed for success in the real world. Engagement occurs when learners can be actively involved in "deep, authentic, and personally relevant learning experiences while also fostering academic achievement, reflection, and civic engagement" (Coiro 2017, 52).

Inquiry-based instruction shifts the roles of teacher and learner, encouraging everyone to learn from everyone. The student acts as an apprentice, and the teacher becomes a guide and coach. Some believe the myth that teachers are needed less as technology teaches more. Actually, the opposite is true—teachers play an even more critical role in helping students learn how to be productive citizens in an increasingly complex and interconnected world.

Some believe the myth that teachers are needed less as technology teaches more. Actually, the opposite is true—teachers play an even more critical role in helping students learn how to be productive citizens in an increasingly complex and interconnected world.

Increases Opportunities for Collaboration

Anyone who has seen students huddled around a screen to seek answers to a question or view an interesting image knows that technology can be social. When students create a shared slideshow for their inquiry project, the process often includes talking through options face-to-face or through online chat if everyone is not in the same room. Technology can bring learners together in many different ways. This social nature of technology lends itself to promoting collaboration among learners, which can lead to deeper learning. "Technology provides opportunities for discussion and collaboration in ways that traditional practices do not always allow" (Conradi 2014, 56). When learners work on a collaborative digital project such as creating a shared document, the edit history reveals a record of their process of co-construction.

Technology can bring learners together in many different ways. This social nature of technology lends itself to promoting collaboration among learners, which can lead to deeper learning.

Collectively working toward a single goal, a hallmark trait of collaboration, hinges on the group's ability to synthesize a myriad of ideas into a cohesive idea of better quality than what one would create alone. When technology enters the mix, research suggests the shared use of a digital tool between two learners can lead to more engagement and deeper learning (Darling-Hammond, Zielezinksi, and Goldman 2014; Hirsh-Pasek et al. 2015).

Collectively working toward a single goal, a hallmark trait of collaboration, hinges on the group's ability to synthesize a myriad of ideas into a cohesive idea of better quality than what one would create alone.

Constructing an understanding can occur through dialogue, as learners seek answers to essential questions, talk through information, listen to more knowledgeable others, and solve problems together (Piaget 1972; Vygotsky 1986). Through this process new knowledge is built for both the speaker and the listener. Unfortunately, in some classrooms, the teacher does most of the talking. Students may come to feel their questions and responses are not valued. But the opposite should be true. Verbalizing their own thoughts may help students organize information and more easily recognize when their view differs from others. When talking through an idea and listening to others, a conceptual shift can occur, leading to the construction of new knowledge (Almasi 1995). In other words, collaborating can deepen understanding. To support this process, the teacher plays a key role by creating a learning environment that supports and encourages questioning, talking, listening, and acceptance of differing views, while also specifically teaching techniques for turn taking, effective listening, sharing ideas, withholding judgment, and acknowledging ideas different from our own.

Through modeling and guided practice, students can become effective collaborators, but let's not kid ourselves, it's not always easy—just as it's not always easy for a grade-level team of teachers to collaborate—but it's important. We know that the social interaction of collaboration, for children and adults, can create a sense of belonging that can lead to engagement, enthusiasm, and active participation in learning (Wu et al. 2013). Once children get excited about learning, they often go beyond talking to finding evidence to support their ideas, then sharing their ideas with others by creating a video, writing a report, or drawing a picture.

The social interaction of collaboration, for children and adults, can create a sense of belonging that can lead to engagement, enthusiasm, and active participation in learning (Wu et al. 2013).

Learning together creates a learning community, which can provide a sense of resilience to support students through challenges and failures. The opposite is also true: feelings of being disconnected, frustrated, or unheard can lead to lower levels of engagement and less learning (Antonio and Guthrie 2008). One research study looked at the conditions needed to support remote collaboration using technology. Researchers compared a group of astrophysicists studying a supernova and a group of eight- to fifteen-year-olds from around the world creating and sharing animated stories and video games. Analysis of chat messages revealed both groups relied on digital tools that supported social creativity, sharing, and play as ways to collaborate on group projects (Aragon et al. 2009). Another study found when students played a video game in person together, sharing one screen, students learned more (Wouters et al. 2013). Collaboration, whether in person or digital, offers opportunities to engage in joint conversations around shared interests, discuss interpretations, make connections, and negotiate differences in thinking.

Effective collaboration with technology stems from skills that can and should specifically be taught to students. In a research study looking at the social collaboration of pairs of third to fifth graders during a structured online inquiry task (Coiro et al. 2014), the students were asked to recommend four eco-friendly toys for the new Green Toy Shop opening in the mall. Twenty-five websites were preselected as resources for the students' search. Researchers found that the pairs who exhibited productive collaboration (1) actively listened; (2) contributed to decisions about navigating online texts; and (3) used prior knowledge to make connections and extend their thinking. Through a back-and-forth manner, the pairs focused on understanding the text and completing the task. Less productive pairs read the text with little discussion, didn't listen actively to each other, and struggled to integrate ideas into their task response. For teachers, when an unproductive team can be identified, supports, such as prompts, can guide students toward stronger collaboration and joint creation of a deeper understanding.

Collaboration skills are life skills. We need more research on the impact of teaching students to collaborate around technology, but the research we do have is promising. One meta-analysis of cooperative learning without technology compared fifty-four articles published from 1995 onward. Cooperative learning was found to positively impact achievement and attitude (Kyndt et al. 2013). If technology can help to create a learning space that promotes collaboration, why wouldn't we use these tools to help our students develop the skills needed for learning, working, and communicating with others? Digital citizenship skills should also be a part of our teaching and embedded within the classroom culture, as students need to know how much information to share online and how to share it effectively.

Encourages Reflection About Learning (Metacognition)

Another important role technology can plan in inquiry-based learning is to foster students' metacognition. Metacognition is often described as "thinking about thinking," but such a simplistic statement almost seems to trivialize this powerful force for building knowledge and deepening learning. Metacognition occurs through reflection—when learners consider their own strategies for learning, monitor how well those strategies work, and adjust the effort needed to learn.

I once had the opportunity to guide a group of students through the process of creating a reflection video using Seesaw, a digital portfolio tool. The third graders spoke about how they and their team learned together during a group inquiry project. It was clear from their heartfelt comments that many had developed an awareness of what they need in order to learn effectively. In literacy learning, metacognition entails evaluating your own sense-making, reorganizing your thinking, and regulating what should occur next in your reading or writing process (Hayes and Flower 1980; Paris, Wasik, and Turner 1991). Reflection is a glimpse of our thought processes, and when these are shared with others, we strengthen our ownership of what we have learned and how we learned it. Research is clear about the value of metacognition in learning (see Hacker, Dunlosky, and Graesser 2009), and cultivating this awareness of how we learn and how much we are learning can lead to higher levels of achievement (Weil et al. 2013).

Reflection about ourselves as learners does not come naturally to everyone, but it's a worthy pursuit. The skills for reflection must be taught directly, modeled, and practiced for students to reflect on learning, celebrate accomplishments, and plan for what comes next. Reflection can be embedded into the inquiry process so that thinking about how and what you learn becomes a natural part of our work as learners. The ultimate goal is for students to display agency, or take charge of their own learning, recognizing that "we construct our understanding of ourselves and the world, we control our thoughts, we monitor the consequences of them" (Hacker, Dunlosky, and Graesser 2009, 1). Students of all ages can benefit from opportunities to deeply consider the impact of their ideas and to take projects through the creation process (Hobbs and Moore 2013). Yet, rather than at the end of a learning process,

Yet, rather than at the end of a learning process, reflecting during the experience can lead to a deeper understanding, more questions, richer discussions, and higher-quality projects.

Technology can encourage reflection and make it visible.

reflecting during the experience can lead to a deeper understanding, more questions, richer discussions, and higher-quality projects.

Technology can encourage reflection and make it visible. Instructional software for reading skills may embed thinking nudges that guide users to pause and consider their strategy use and also prompt effective strategy use based on the students' performance (Yehudit et al. 2018). More research is needed to help us know if students actually take the software's advice, put the thinking strategies into practice, and make learning gains. Tech tools, such as Flipgrid, Seesaw, and screencasting applications, make reflection visible as learners video record thoughts about their learning and share these with others.

Builds Background Knowledge and Media Literacy Skills

Background, or prior knowledge, shapes the ways students make sense of new information—a critical part of inquiry. Jean Piaget's neuroscience research (1972) helps us understand how the brain forms connections between bits of information as new knowledge is constructed and stored in the brain's logical information storage system or schema. Multimedia, including videos, podcasts, graphics, text, and animations, can provide a boost or quicken the pace of acquiring background knowledge. Visual literacy skills are a key foundation for students to make meaning from images, critically analyze the messages within photos, videos, and other media, and to use this information to solve a problem or create a project.

For information on teaching students how to "read" multimedia texts, see Section 3, pages 59–60.

The cognitive theory of multimedia learning (Mayer and Moreno 1998) stems from the idea that two key channels of brain learning are visual (images, written text, animation, videos) and verbal (spoken narration). Meaningful learning, the building of background knowledge, occurs when both paths are utilized at the same time. A video with captions or print with an audiobook lets a reader use two pathways for learning. However, the research of Mayer and Moreno shows that more is not necessarily better, and there can be a point where too many options impede learning.

Spoken text with images is an effective way of sharing information, but if animation is added, then the cognitive load may be too much for the learner. The additional pathway may serve as a distraction rather than a support.

A video with captions or print with an audiobook lets a reader use two pathways for learning. However, the research of Mayer and Moreno shows that more is not necessarily better, and there can be a point where too many options impede learning.

When using multimedia resources with students, strive to locate and create quality resources that maximize learning, but be aware of how multimedia presents information to avoid overload or distraction. A team of researchers set out to understand the ways multimedia resources can best meet the learning needs of students. The team concluded that a student's amount of background knowledge impacted the time it took to understand multimedia (X. Yang et al. 2018). Learners with high background knowledge spent more time reading and viewing the new information and more time transitioning between graphics and text. On the other hand, students with low background knowledge needed more instruction to develop a coherence between their knowledge and the new information in the multimedia resources. This finding led to the conclusion that when multimedia resources build in prompts to help viewers access and build background knowledge, learning is more successful. Additionally, many students can benefit from a teacher's explicit prompts to link new information to their background knowledge. As always, effective use of the technology relies on quality instruction from the teacher.

Consider how *you* use technology to build background knowledge. How-to videos guide viewers through the steps of a project, getting the brain ready for the actual hands-on experience useful for constructing knowledge (Goodyear and Retalis 2010). It's likely if you want to begin a new hobby, the internet is one of your first stops. When I wanted to learn how to crochet a scarf, I went online to read about crocheting, see diagrams of different sizes of hooks, and view tutorial videos. With some practice, I was soon on the way to my first crochet project. Technology supported me as I learned a new skill, but I really took off when I sat down with my aunt, a master crocheter, who gave me specific feedback about my work. The combination of

A student's amount of background knowledge impacted the time it took to understand multimedia (X. Yang et al. 2018). Learners with high background knowledge spent more time reading and viewing the new information and more time transitioning between graphics and text. On the other hand, students with low background knowledge needed more instruction to develop a coherence between their knowledge and the new information in the multimedia resources.

tech's knowledge-building opportunities and a teacher's instruction is key.

We want students' background knowledge to grow in ways that lead to developing an understanding of new information—to learn. Yet multimedia resources, possibly more so than print resources, are influenced by popular culture, mass media, and social media. Media literacy skills are critical for students' understanding of what they see and hear in multimedia resources. The National Association for Media Literacy Education defines media literacy as "the ability to access, analyze, evaluate, and communicate information in a variety of forms including print and nonprint messages" (n.d.) Thinking critically about the messages they receive and create is imperative for our students, as they prepare for their future role as voting citizens. Research suggests explicitly teaching media literacy skills can lead to improvements in critical thinking about bias and misinformation in messages, and an understanding that people interpret media in different ways (Jeong, Cho, and Hwang 2012; Kahne and Bowyer 2017; Webb and Martin 2012).

Teachers can support students' development of media literacy skills by embedding instruction amidst inquiry-based lessons. Teach students to

- identify the creator, the purpose, and the point of view of a resource. Build students' capacities for understanding how messages are constructed and the assumptions on which messages are built (Hobbs and Moore 2013).
- sort fact from fiction by defining and using terms accurately (e.g., *fake news, misleading news, false news, propaganda, hoax, sponsored content*). Utilize the infographic "Beyond 'Fake News' 10—Types of Misleading News" as a reliable source for developing these concepts (Hobbs 2017; Steinberg 2017).

Although media literacy concepts may seem complex, developing critical analysis skills can begin at an early age. I work with a kindergarten teacher who uses a shared reading time to focus on teaching fact and opinion. Students are introduced to a website that sells products and one that only provides information. Together, she and the students discern which website is fact and which is opinion. As children become older, the focus can shift to identifying hidden messages and considering the value of multimedia within the social, political, and cultural climate of the time.

For guidelines on media literacy, including evaluating bias, see Section 3 pages 61-64.

Enhances the Process and Products of Writing

A critical element of inquiry entails sharing new learning with others. When our words reach the eyes and ears of others, we feel empowered. Technology can facilitate this process. For some, word processing, as opposed to writing by hand, is more motivating and leads to longer and better pieces of writing (see Figure 2–6). Not only do word processing programs make the revision process easy, often additional support tools are embedded, including spell check, formatting, voice recognition, and text to speech. Word processing tools, whether used to write a text message or a research paper, can remove roadblocks and make writing more fluid.

FIGURE 2–6 *The Advantages of Word Processing*

The Advantages of Word Processing over Writing by Hand

- The quality and length of writing improves (see Graham and Perin 2007).
- Reluctant writers may be more engaged (Goldberg, Russell, and Cook 2003).
- For weak writers, the development/organization of the text improves (see Morphy and Graham 2012).
- For students with learning disabilities, instruction combined with word processing leads to higher-quality writing (MacArthur 2006).

Instructional software for writing skills can take word processing to the next level. A supportive gamelike environment uses animated characters to give visual and textual clues as the student creates a piece of writing within the instructional program. The software provides feedback on how well the student's written summary matches the exemplar text (Little et al. 2018). In the future, artificial intelligence may be refined enough to provide individual students with targeted instruction, but to date, the teacher remains the best source of guidance for composing text.

When word processing tools *replace* paper and pencil, the physical way we write changes, but the finished product is similar —a collection of written words. But technology can *transform* writing when digital text, images, video, and audio are layered into the writing process. Writing with media, also known as multimedia composition or digital writing, reflects the ways language, culture, and technology interact.

Research in the area of writing and technology can guide teachers seeking ways to encourage students to express information and their ideas in multiple ways. In a review of twenty-nine empirical studies published from 2002 to 2017, researchers drew the following conclusions about digital writing: (1) instruction on digital writing improved students' composing processes and writing skills; (2) technology motivated students to participate in writing activities; (3) digital writing increased social interaction and peer collaboration (Williams and Beam 2019).

Not long ago I had the chance to see these findings in action with a fourth-grade teacher who gave her students a writing assignment to create a meme about the importance of persistence in learning. First, she explained memes and how they convey ideas, then she asked the students to use Creative Commons to locate copyright-free images and work in pairs to write a phrase of three to eight words to convey their idea, which they did enthusiastically. The writing activity gave students the chance to use a writing form from popular culture and to explore the social/emotional aspect of learning, while also developing digital writing skills. Another teacher at the same building, an elementary STEM (science, technology, engineering, and mathematics) facilitator for second graders, asked the students to work in pairs to keep a digital science journal. First, he assigned research partners to collect data from the school garden through images, videos, measurements, and written observations. Through this multimedia composition, the students created a research record rich in details. In both of these classrooms, technology broadened the traditional views of what writing is and how it's created and gave students meaningful activities for developing their digital writing skills.

Technology opens up a world of possibilities for students not only to create a message, but also to share their ideas with others. This ease of sharing is a fundamental difference between traditional writing and digital writing. We have long known that words have power, convey information, and carry emotions, but with technology, words have the potential to reach a broader audience. Technology-based writing tools can facilitate idea sharing and spark creativity by

- broadening the audience beyond just the teacher (Block and Strachan 2019)
- encouraging more writing in a wider variety of formats (Mills and Exley 2014)
- promoting collaboration (Purcell, Buchanan, and Friedrich 2013).

We have long known that words have power, convey information, and carry emotions, but with technology, words have the potential to reach a broader audience.

All of these can promote engagement in the writing process, especially when students see the impact their writing has on others. For example, if a student writes a blog post encouraging school families to recycle, a count of those who accessed the post, as well as a count of those who attended the school recycling event, provide evidence of a blog post's impact. In this way digital writing helps students develop a sense that their ideas are worthwhile, what they have to say matters, and they can make a difference in their community.

Using technology to create and share writing fundamentally changes the landscape of writing. Writers of all ages must be more keenly aware of copyright issues, internet safety, and digital etiquette, as these issues complicate writing beyond the basic print text. A teacher's role remains critical in guiding students through these challenges.

Digital Games for Literacy Learning

Technology requires us to constantly assess new tools against what we know to be true about education and effective instructional practices. For example, John Dewey, in his writings from the early 1900s, advocated for students to actively take part in their own learning. He believed school should be a place where students learned content and real-world skills. Dewey's ideas ring true today as shifts in pedagogy and practices seek to utilize technology to support students' active learning by enhancing the inquiry process.

Outside of school, many students cite video games as their favorite pastime, and yet their use in education has been limited. Can a game support the kind of authentic inquiry we know supports learning? Effective use of technology game-based learning can be a way for students to practice facts and develop literacy skills, such as spelling, vocabulary, or literal comprehension. One research study found that 79 percent of young people who play video games read game-related materials on a monthly basis, including in-game communications, game reviews, and game-related books, blogs, and fan fiction. In addition, one-third of young game players believe playing video games makes them a better reader (Picton, Clark, and Judge 2020). A systematic review of research about video games and learning shows the most common use of video games is to acquire knowledge (Boyle et al. 2016). Digital learning games may include virtual worlds, simulations, interactive stories, and practice/quiz activities. The positive effect digital games have on learning stems from the games' very nature: visual and interactive (Boyle et al. 2016). A meta-analysis of seventy-seven research studies found serious video games to be more effective for learning and retention than conventional methods of instruction, and students learned more when the games were combined with other instructional methods (Wouters et al. 2013). Elementary teachers identify the benefits

Can a game support the kind of authentic inquiry we know supports learning? Effective use of technology game-based learning can be a way for students to practice facts and develop literacy skills, such as spelling, vocabulary, or literal comprehension.

of computer games as leading to engagement, providing individualized practice, and giving feedback for learning (Proctor and Marks 2013). Quality learning games create active learners, so the best games promote active exploration of virtual worlds, along with emphasizing self-direction and choice.

Quality learning games create active learners, so the best games promote active exploration of virtual worlds, along with emphasizing self-direction and choice.

Vivid visual scenes and rich sound environments hook players, making serious games *appear* to be motivating for students. Extrinsic motivation may drive students to gain points or level up, but some believe digital game-based activities are only dressing up the drill-and-practice activities typically found in a spelling workbook or set of high-frequency word flashcards. When games use the behaviorist ideas of repetition and reinforcement (Bruner 1960), game tasks can promote learning but also can become routine. Students may figure out how to "game" the game, developing shortcuts around the game and around any hope of deep and lasting learning. While visiting a school, I observed a fourth grader, Nathan, playing a reading comprehension game on his tablet during a literacy station time. The game required a minimum play time of twenty minutes. Nathan figured out that if he sat with his tablet open and occasionally selected a random response, he could wait out the twenty minutes, then close the tablet. Although the results of his work were available to his teacher, she focused her attention on other aspects of classroom teaching and learning. She viewed the literacy game, a requirement of the school district, as a time filler, and so did Nathan.

For many educators, the benefits of digital games outweigh the drawbacks, but making this judgment requires us to know our learning goals and purpose for using the digital games, recognize what our students need, and decide if digital games are a good choice for meeting our goals. When our goal is to promote deep thinking, video games may be a viable option. Look for games that balance the challenges with just doable activities (not too easy, not too hard, just right) (Gee 2003), make content interesting, and add a dose of fun that can lead to the intrinsic motivation needed for lasting learning. But be careful about assuming that all children are motivated by video games. An analysis of studies researching the motivational effects of serious games found games are not any more motivational than traditional instruction (Wouters et al. 2013). Research shared in this section helps us to understand video games are not a one-size-fits-all approach to learning. For some students learning some skills in some settings, video games can be an effective way to utilize technology to promote learning.

Technology Paired with Instruction Works Best

Intentional is the key word for integrating technology into instruction. Let's zoom in on one study of K–12 classrooms conducted by researchers Cheung and Slavin (2011) to see the effect of pairing a teacher's instruction with technology. This meta-analysis was selected because it examined a large number of studies (eighty-five) over an extended amount of time (forty years, from 1970 to 2010). All the studies met stringent quantitative research criteria, including the use of experimental and control groups. Comparisons of results across the studies led researchers to the following conclusions:

- Instructional technology produced a positive but small effect on reading achievement.
- No significant difference in reading achievement was found when teaching with a technology-based program.
- Technology-based reading instruction had more positive impact on what the researchers defined as low ability and English language learners than on high-ability students.
- The largest effects occured in programs that paired technology-based activities with traditional reading instructional activities (i.e., shared reading, skills lessons, small-group instruction, modeled and independent reading).
- More technology did not necessarily result in better outcomes. Results showed little difference between low-intensity (fifteen minutes or less a day) and high-intensity (more than fifteen minutes a day) programs.

Results of this meta-analysis indicate that integrating technology into reading instruction can lead to a slight increase in reading achievement for some aspects of reading, for some students. Researchers point out three limitations of the study: (1) only studies with quantitative measures of reading were examined, leaving out other perspectives; (2) only programs used in a school setting for at least twelve weeks were examined, leaving out programs of a shorter duration; and (3) standardized tests were primarily used to measure reading achievement, even though alternative assessments can yield valuable insight about reading achievement. A key conclusion from this study is that the pairing of reading instruction with technology-based activities is necessary for improving reading achievement.

Universal Design for Learning with Technology

The Universal Design for Learning (UDL) model creates true differentiated instruction based on individual learners' needs. Universal Design for Learning principles focus on designing instruction that includes representing information in multiple ways, choice, modeling, scaffolding, feedback about correctness, and nudges to continue, which can lead to more effective in-person and online instructional activities (Rose and Meyer 2002). Gone are the days of pulling out the tablets simply because it's Friday afternoon, the day before a holiday, or only a few minutes before dismissal. UDL encourages teachers to consider the "shades of strength and weakness that make each [learner] unique" (2002, 11) and utilize the powerful flexibility of technology to design effective instruction. By matching tech tools to students' learning needs, access becomes a priority rather than an afterthought.

Universal Design for Learning (UDL) principles focus on designing instruction that includes representing information in multiple ways, choice, modeling, scaffolding, feedback about correctness, and nudges to continue, which can lead to more effective in-person and online instructional activities.

Digital texts, whether read on a computer, tablet, or cell phone, give readers multiple means of representing the text: customize the display, add an audio option with the text, highlight important information, access a built-in dictionary, and in some cases even vary the difficulty level of the vocabulary. Technology can provide access to information in ways that traditional print cannot, removing barriers and making learning within reach for more learners. An e-book's font can be enlarged or backlight added to enable reading for those with limited vision. With an audiobook, a student can listen to a text at a higher level of comprehension than they can read, and a podcast presents ideas in a convenient, portable format. Screen reader software lets a reader access a digital text visually and auditorily.

Tech tools, such as interactive presentation tools and clickers, can vary the ways students respond during the lesson and promote engagement and active participation. Pear Deck and Nearpod are examples of interactive presentation tools that give students the opportunity to interact with information displayed by the teacher but accessed on their individual devices. These tools present information through words, images, video, and audio, and students can respond through multiple-choice or open-ended questions, and even draw a response to submit. Student responses can remain anonymous to the class, but not to the teacher, and can provide a wealth of informal assessment data a teacher can use to guide instruction.

Assistive technologies provide access through captioning, voice recognition, and text to speech. These tools can benefit students no matter their learning needs. Graphic organizer and mind-mapping tools (e.g., Coggle and Popplet) guide students through the process of organizing their ideas, and digital drawing tools let students express their ideas in an alternative format. Translation software can help students acquiring a second language to focus on content in their first language when needed.

Choice is a powerful motivator, and tech tools provide access to more titles and formats of text, allowing students to choose based on their own interests and the grade-level curriculum. Epic, Vooks, and PebbleGo provide access to digital texts that align with student interests and reading abilities. Some digital texts, such as the ones on the website Newsela, offer similar content at varying difficulty levels, letting students access information in a way that best meets their learning needs, which can increase engagement.

A move from using technology for consuming information to creating content lets students express what they have learned in creative ways. Visual presentations can be created with digital slides or an interactive presentation tool, such as Prezi. Audio and visual images can work in sync to share information (e.g., Prezi, Flipgrid, iMovie). Teaching students various ways to show what they know lets all learners create projects that reflect new learning utilizing their personal, creative style. Digital tools can also provide ways to develop project timelines and capture the brainstorming ideas (e.g., mindmapping apps and websites) that are critical for the creation process.

In addition, software designed with the UDL principles can create an individualized learning experience that leads to the development of reading comprehension and word knowledge skills, especially for students who struggle with reading or are learning English (Coyne et al. 2012; Hall et al. 2015; Proctor, Dalton, and Grisham 2007). Building the UDL principles into our own instruction and selecting resources with built-in features based on the principles are two ways teachers can ensure technology's effective use for learners' literacy growth.

The Technology Integration Planning Cycle

The Technology Integration Planning Cycle presents technology integration as a circular sequence, with the instructional goal being the beginning and end point (see Figure 2–7). The planning cycle was created based on the results of a series of research studies analyzing teachers' uses of technology in literacy teaching (Hutchison, Beschorner, and Schmidt-Crawford 2012; Hutchison and Reinking 2011). Two points along the planning cycle circle provide for opting out of technology integration if a nondigital option seems best or if the constraints of technology detract from learning. There could be times when technology isn't the right choice. A key point of the Technology Integration Planning Cycle is that you decide if and when technology benefits learning and how technology should be used—and those decisions occur intentionally.

When working with a group of fourth graders, I designed a digital research activity for students to search on preselected websites for information about tornadoes. The students summarized what they learned on a paper poster because we just didn't have enough time to add learning how to use a digital creation tool to this lesson. But the next time we did a research project, the students knew the process, so we could devote time to learning a digital tool and integrate it into our lesson. For our original lesson, a digital tool (online text) supported our nondigital work. At other times a paper tool (print book) may support digital work (creating a podcast).

The Technology Integration Planning Cycle (Figure 2–7) presents a model that emphasizes a teacher's decision-making process for integrating technology. The cycle calls for teachers to

1. select learning goals connected to standards (instructional goal)
2. make pedagogical decisions about instructional approaches (e.g., small group vs. whole class; more teacher centered vs. more student centered) (instructional approach)
3. identify tools and resources (tool selection)
4. specify how the digital tool is the best fit for the instructional goal (contribution to instruction)
5. identify limitations of the digital tool (constraints).

Using a guide to walk through the decision-making process is helpful for teachers new to integrating technology into literacy instruction, but even experienced teachers can benefit from pausing to consider the fit of a digital tool to the instructional goal.

FIGURE 2–7 *Technology Integration Planning Cycle for Literacy* (Hutchinson, A.C. and Woodward, L. 2014)

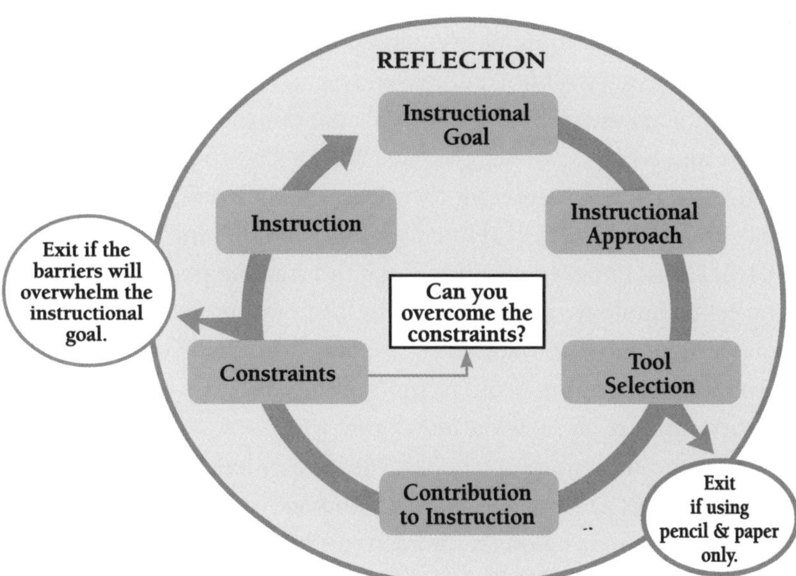

Guidelines for Choosing and Using Technology Tools

New digital tools appear, while other digital tools go by the wayside—it can be hard to keep up! Yet it's important for teachers to look beyond the bells and whistles of what the tool can do and focus on what the *students* can do with the digital tool to meet the learning goals. Shifting the focus lets us more easily adapt when our favorite digital tool charges a fee or is no longer available. We simply search for another tool that lets us work in a similar way.

One study in an elementary school (McDermott and Gormley 2015) found that teachers most commonly use digital tools to

- display multimedia content
- generate interactive learning activities
- focus student attention

- display texts for shared reading
- individualize students' learning activities

Although this study only explored the digital teaching practices at one elementary school, additional research shows elementary-aged students use technology to consume information (i.e., reading online and e-books, viewing videos) rather than to produce information as a way to represent their learning (i.e., writing a blog post, creating a podcast) (Hutchison, Woodward, and Colwell 2016). Consuming information is a good starting point for integrating technology into teaching, but it's not a place to rest on our laurels. We want our students to be active learners. Producing information by creating projects and multimodal texts gives students opportunities to show what they know.

In some classrooms, technology is used in less active and engaging ways as students get older. Younger students might share the pen when writing on an interactive whiteboard, and older students might take a quiz or practice skills within the school's online reading program (McDermott and Gormley 2015). Literacy instruction for middle and high school students mostly utilizes digital tools to read and write multimodal texts, collaborate, collect resources, and share and solicit feedback (Hutchison and Colwell 2014). Although this isn't always the case, as students gain more knowledge and experience and their ability to analyze information develops, we would want students to use technology to support these deeper ways of thinking. Choosing and using digital tools should be based on the value technology can add to a teacher's instructional practices and the students' learning (Mishra and Koehler 2006). A teacher can select appropriate digital tools when planning instruction by considering the learning needs of students, the goals and objectives of the curriculum, the features of the tech tool, and the teacher's ability to adapt the tool to fit the learning (Okojie, Olinzock, and Okojie-Boulder 2006).

Begin by deciding what to teach and effective ways to teach it. This pinpoints the focus of the lesson on the content, rather than the digital tool. Next, select a digital tool that lets students work in the way that best matches the lesson. If needed, make adaptations to fit the tool to the lesson. James Ritter's fifth graders researched the inquiry question: Who were key figures during the Revolutionary War time, and how did their actions influence our lives today? Together, he and the students brainstormed people and located biographies in the school library and on the internet. Students worked in pairs to read, synthesize, take notes, then create a digital presentation to share during a family literacy showcase event. During the creation process, James asked students to first focus on the content of their presentation. Decisions about the visual aspects (color, font, graphics) would come after he reviewed their work. James knew his students had the tendency to spend lots of time searching for images online or changing font and background color, rather than deepening their knowledge about the topic. For this reason he adapted the tool to fit his students' learning needs by having students first use the word-processing feature, then the visual tools.

Where Does Technology Lead Us Now?

Growth with technology integration is a process. There may be days of technology mishaps—where a device won't turn on, three keys fall off a keyboard, the internet stops working for five days in a row, or you have to stop teaching because a student is viewing inappropriate images—all real technology problems I have experienced in schools! But none of these are valid reasons for not integrating technology into our teaching. There will also be days when everything works like clockwork and your students amaze you by what they are capable of doing and learning with technology. Either way we must continue to move forward, both individually and as a field. This can be difficult to do.

For as much as we know about integrating technology into education, questions about its effectiveness continually emerge, and hopefully future research will help us find answers. As new generations of technological tools emerge, the big question for us, and maybe you too, continues to be: Which technologies, implemented in which ways and for what duration, lead to deep and lasting learning? In addition, we know that gamification and artificial intelligence present interesting ways of thinking about how technology can support learning. Also, after our experiences with teaching during a pandemic, we can't help but wonder how online learning may change our role as teachers in both the face-to-face and virtual classroom.

Although these questions linger in the corner of our minds, subtle and seismic shifts toward integrating technology in teaching and learning occur in classrooms every day. Section 3 focuses on the experiences of Suzanne, myself, and teachers we know who are open to exploring ways to bring quality instruction and technology together.

SECTION **3**

BUT THAT

Responsive Planning of Technology for Literacy Learning

SUZANNE KELLY AND ELIZABETH DOBLER

If you walked into Suzanne's classroom recently, to observe, every student would not be sitting alone at a desk, eyes on a computer screen, headphones on. Instead, some hold traditional paper books, paper, and writing utensils; others read from tablets or write on a laptop. Some students record their thinking with sticky notes and notebooks, pens poised to draw and jot notes and questions. Other students use their device to record notes into a shared doc for their reading club. A few wear headphones as they listen to an audiobook, their eyes following the printed words in a book. All students are reading and writing using the tools that make it possible for them to do their best work. As students work, Suzanne moves throughout the room, conferring with individual and grouped students, and occasionally checking into the classroom drive to see students' writing and reflections on their reading. This is a thriving, literacy-rich classroom that, although looking effortless, actually reflects careful planning of how, when, and whether to use technology. As Beth explained in Section 2, in the most intentional literacy instruction, technology is a tool that is used flexibly to enhance individual and collective learning.

The way school looked during the height of the COVID-19 pandemic reinforced many people's perceptions that most students do not thrive sitting in front of a computer all day. Without relationships and the microaffirmations of daily feedback, many students' learning engagement waned. Work got completed but in the most cursory compliant way. In the chaos of our transition from live to virtual learning, even the best teachers understandably defaulted to some ineffective uses of tech based on coverage of content area topics and not necessarily on the quality of the pedagogy. As all of us learned, good use of technology must be anchored to what we know about healthy teaching and learning. When it is, and teachers have the time to explore options and plan for their specific students and curriculum goals, technology can be a valuable helpmate for

- using shared drives and documents to optimize peer collaboration
- using recorded audio and video clips to give feedback
- increasing the use of digital texts to expand text choices
- using video conference capabilities to make connections with families
- recording key lessons that students can watch and rewatch as needed
- normalizing the use of accessibility capabilities like dictation and translation software, audiobooks, and closed captioning
- sharing cohosting or coteaching duties with a student to help keep things moving if the tech breaks down.

Intentionality Is Critical

When you consider your own classroom or school and the role technology currently plays, our guess is that a few things come to mind. You might start first with your hopes for the integration of technology into literacy instruction—such as building students' background knowledge or giving them access to a wider array of texts. And as you start to get excited about the possibilities, you might also naturally begin to consider the obstacles, such as the digital divide, finding and curating quality resources, concerns about too much screen time leading to isolation, and more. The good news is that all of this can be addressed with some forethought and planning. One does not just stumble into great literacy instruction that is well integrated with technology. Rather, by keeping our goals, our concerns, and what research has shown us at the forefront, we will be well positioned for success.

That kind of planning with technology first and foremost involves questions about access.

Addressing the Digital Divide

In the perfect world, everyone would be able to access digital learning anytime they needed. Access would not be limited by cost or location—but, as you know, this perfect world does not yet exist. When we think about unequal access to technology, we think beyond yes-or-no to the range of access students have. (See Figure 3–1.)

FIGURE 3–1 *Range of Student Access to Technology*

- **Full access:** Students have consistent digital access (a highly functioning computer and reliable internet) and adult support in applying the full potential of those tools meaningfully.
- **Partial access:** Students have unreliable (some) access to a device and the internet and little to no adult support in navigating the tools.
- **No access:** Students don't have digital access.

Technology is so much a part of our daily lives that it can be easy for us to assume what kind of access other people have. And we really can't assume. Socioeconomics might play a role but even if a family has Wi-Fi or devices, there might be multiple family members who are using them, strict screen time limits, or other family obligations that interfere with students accessing the technology. Too often students and families are put in the position of having to problem solve technology gaps related to school work on their own, and this often means that those students and families are labeled as "disengaged" when in fact they may have the will but not the tools for engagement. Going beyond yes-or-no to asking what kind of device and internet access students have helps teachers anticipate challenges students may have when completing work at home. See Figure 3–2 for a family survey on digital access and Figure 3–3 for some problem-solving scenarios.

As Beth explained in Section 2, our concern about inequal access to technology is about access to opportunity and whether or not students gain competency with the tools expected of them in the larger society.

FIGURE 3–2 *Family Survey for Digital Access*

1. What kinds of devices does the child have easy access to at home? (We ask this question to best identify which programs the child can use for learning. This means your student would need to be able to use the device any time during learning hours.)
   - Cell phone—indicate make and model
   - Laptop/tablet—indicate make and model
   - Video game console—indicate make and model
   - No device
2. Does the child share a device with other family members? How much access to the device can the child expect each day?
3. Does the child have internet access? If so, what speed: high speed, medium, basic? (We ask this question to understand whether the child has easy access to streaming content.)
4. What does the child use devices to do at home? (There is no right answer. We want to learn from all the ways students engage with technology.)
   - Play games—what games?
   - Read—e-books, websites . . . ?
   - Use apps—YouTube, Facebook, Instagram, TikTok . . . ? For what purposes? (Watch gaming videos, comedy, dance, follow celebrities, learn how to make things . . . please be as specific as possible in your answers.)
   - The child doesn't use devices.
   - Other:
5. Does the child encounter any problems while using technology (such as the internet frequently freezing)?
6. Is there something you or the child wishes they could do using technology?

FIGURE 3–3 *Common Problems and Solutions for Digital Access*

PROBLEM	POSSIBLE SOLUTIONS
Lagging device: The older a device is, the more lagging becomes a problem. This is particularly true for tablets and cell phones. A computer that is four years old may be fine but a four-year-old cell phone or tablet may lag too much to be of use for any except the simplest tasks.	Instead of using a computer program that requires students to do their work, email/text/print the assignment and give students the option of doing the work by hand. Students can turn in the work by texting a photograph of the handwritten work or hand it in when in class.
Lack of one-to-one devices in school: Although many schools have computer labs or carts that can be rotated among classrooms, some don't have enough devices for one class.	Consider planning rotating computer use during independent work time. Plan when each student will use the device so that every student has access on a regular basis. Plan targeted conferring around tech use to make sure students' time with the device is as productive as possible.
Assigning work that requires digital access: Up to 70% of teachers assign homework that requires online access (McLaughlin 2016) and yet we can't assume that students can get onto the internet during specific hours at home.	First, consider creating a no-tech version of every assignment. We understand that a no-tech version of every assignment might not seem reasonable particularly when you plan for students to share their work using a specific digital platform. If that's the case, then consider how the students might work on the assignment over time so that they could choose to do the technology component during independent work time in class and use their homework time for another activity, like reading a print book. That flexibility is key to making sure no student feels locked out of an essential experience.

(continues)

(continued)

PROBLEM	POSSIBLE SOLUTIONS
Self-management: For students who are used to doing work in the social, peer, and teacher-supportive environment of a classroom, working with technology on their own can lead to disengagement.	Create opportunities for online collaboration by giving students the option of working together or assigning that expectation. Email students reminders of how they can be managing their time, and make yourself available for help if needed.

Whenever you share a digital tool for learning or ask students to create digital content, consider what type of access is needed and its availability in the situation. Creating and sharing video/audio projects (such as Adobe Spark or iMovie) takes more bandwidth than a slide presentation (such as Google Slides or PowerPoint) or a visual storytelling platform (such as Prezi or Powtoon). See Figure 3–4 for some ways of assessing online activities based on download speed.

FIGURE 3–4 *Recommended Download Speed Per One User for Online Activities*

ACTIVITY	BROADBAND SPEED (MBPS)
Searching the web	1
Checking email	.05–1
Downloading instructional materials, including open educational resources	1
Engaging with social media	.03
Completing multiple-choice assessments	.06
Sharing cloud-based documents (Office 365, Google Apps)	50
Steaming music	2
Streaming video—standard-definition quality—ultra-high-density quality	3–25

ACTIVITY	BROADBAND SPEED (MBPS)
Streaming high-density video or lecture	4
Watching a video conference	1
Collaborating in a video conference	1
Engaging with simulation and gaming	1
Engaging in two-way online gaming	4

Fox, C., Jones, R. 2016. *The Broadband Imperative II: Equitable Access for Learning.* Washington, D.C.: State Educational Technology Directors Association (SETDA).

These problem-solving tools can't cover every scenario. That's why we emphasize the importance of teacher-family and teacher-student ongoing communication. We need to think beyond whether students are getting the work done to what the process is like for them. Some students might not be working to their full potential because of a struggle with the tools for learning, and we won't know unless we actively inquire. Before we engage in using technology, we often ask students, "What might be challenging for you or others in getting this done?" Often, when we make this a group discussion, one student will articulate another student's unspoken concerns. And after students complete the work, we ask them, "Was there anything in the process of completing this work that you struggled with? Let's talk together to figure out how we can make that easier next time."

We need to think beyond whether students are getting the work done to what the process is like for them.

Before we engage in using technology, we often ask students, "What might be challenging for you or others in getting this done?"

If you sense access might be getting in the way of learning, back down a step or two and rely on lower-tech activities, such as a discussion board with images or a collaborative document, rather than streaming video. If you can't ensure everyone will be successful, consider whether technology is critical for students to develop an understanding during this activity. Be sure to have a plan B for kids who do not have the access to tech or who have a device that might be outdated, and offer students the choice of using tech or not. Although it is true that tech might be the easiest or most efficient option, digital devices are simply a ramped-up version of analogue tools humans have been using for years. So, for example, if the goal is for students' written work to reach a wider audience, blogging or a class website might feel like the best ways to accomplish those goals; however, finished pieces can also be photocopied and distributed, including several copies placed in the school library. They can also be bound together in a class anthology of work, with each student taking home a copy. We might be tempted to think every student must use digital slides to augment their oral presentation, but students can also hone their visual presentation skills through poster boards and gestures, while using paper notecards to plan what to say. For activities like book trailers or other video-recorded work, live presentation can be just as powerful. When teaching about social media content use, such as crowd sourcing, you can show students that shared digital docs and social media are helpful, but so too are the original crowd source forms like community bulletin boards and roundtable brainstorming sessions. Only after you've determined issues of access can you plan for literacy teaching with technology. For further resources on bridging the digital divide, see Figure 3–5.

If you can't ensure everyone will be successful, consider whether technology is critical for students to develop an understanding during this activity.

FIGURE 3–5 *Further Resources for Bridging the Digital Divide*

- **Organizations providing families with computers and technology training** (Network for Good n.d.): https://www.networkforgood.org/topics/education/digitaldivide/
- **How to help families access low-cost and free internet, devices, and educational content** (Fazlullah 2020): https://www.commonsense.org/education/articles/5-ways-to-get-all-students-connected-for-distance-learning
- **List of educational apps that don't need wi-fi or data** (Common Sense Media n.d.): https://www.commonsensemedia.org/lists/educational-apps-that-dont-need-wi-fi-or-data

Will Technology Deepen Students' Learning Experience?

When you next feel the inevitable intimidation that you or your students *must* use a specific digital tool, remind yourself that technology is the tool, not the driver. Skilled teachers make intentional choices about whether, when, what for, and how to use technology based on the curriculum and their specific students. Use Figure 3–6 to consider when technology deepens your students' learning.

When you next feel the inevitable intimidation that you or your students must *use a specific digital tool, remind yourself that technology is the tool, not the driver.*

FIGURE 3–6 *Technology Decision-Making Guidelines for Teachers*

QUESTIONS TO GUIDE DECISION-MAKING	TECHNOLOGY TOOLS THAT CAN DEEPEN LEARNING
Does the technology increase access to information?	Search engines, databases, websites, video tutorials, podcasts, e-books
Does the technology make information accessible?	Personalized font size, back lighting, highlighting, built-in dictionary, text to speech and speech to text, screen readers, closed caption, translation
Does the technology support knowledge creation?	Mind-mapping software, video collaboration, document sharing tools, project creation tools
Does the technology promote reflection about one's learning?	Screencasting tools, video/audio recording tools

These questions help us avoid the bad habit of always defaulting to one tech tool by considering the best choices for the *specific content and students*. We can't assume that all kids would rather use a device and that all kids *know how* to use these apps and devices. When we make these assumptions, we are at the very least eliminating students' agency as learners and often putting

We can't assume that all kids would rather use a device and that all kids know how to use these apps and devices.

them in situations where they're not set up to succeed. Outside of school our students use technology for entertainment and communication, but just because a student has a cell phone doesn't mean they are adept at using technology for learning. Students need us to model that decision-making about whether a specific tool serves the content's purpose and to give them opportunities to practice it on their own.

The interactive whiteboard provides an easy way to explore new tech with students. Not only does this help them learn a process of inquiry into new tech but also shows that adults, teachers, and students are always learning about new tech and questioning whether it's worthwhile for our purposes. This process of metacognition is useful not just for how we model using tech for learning but also for our own relationship with technology. As adults, we all know how easy it is to fall into unconscious habits with technology. We want students to be the opposite of mindless, as learners and consumers. See Figure 3–7 for prompts students and teachers can use to explore tech.

As adults, we all know how easy it is to fall into unconscious habits with technology. We want students to be the opposite of mindless, as learners and consumers.

As Beth made clear in Section 2, accessible and working technology is a start, but it is not enough. A teacher needs to have a strong knowledge of literacy goals, outside of the technology realm, to know how to utilize digital tools to their best advantage.

While observing student book clubs recently, I (Suzanne) noticed one club, The Book Worms, using sentence stems ("I think . . ."; "I agree with you because . . ."; "I disagree with you because . . .") but not adding the details necessary to have a robust discussion about their book. When I sat down to ask how their book talks were going, the students knew the conversation wasn't going as well as it could. I started to ask the kinds of questions that would help us collaboratively plan for a better outcome. What, I wondered, do they usually do when they feel stuck in book talks? The group explained that they had already turned to their book talk checklist and rubric for ideas but that had only pointed them

FIGURE 3–7 *Self-Directed Inquiry into Technology*

- **Why am I excited about this tech?** Engagement matters.
- **What is the purpose of my task? How does the tech support that purpose?** If students aren't clear about the task's purpose, they won't use any tool well, tech or not.
- **Am I confident using this tech? Will the time it takes to use the tool interfere with me completing the task?** Student work, in and outside of school, is time sensitive. We need to schedule opportunities for students to explore new tech with no formal assessment of content so that students master the tool before applying it to content-heavy contexts. Using tech can increase disengagement from learning if students are frustrated navigating the tool.
- **How can I make sure the tech doesn't take over the task/distract us from the work we need to do?** We have all seen a PowerPoint so overcrowded with animation and sounds that we're distracted from the content. Or we've had the experience of sitting down with our cell phone or computer to complete one short task and then realizing two hours later that we got distracted by all the possibilities of the tool (and never completed our original task). Much of the technology we use is designed to keep us using that specific tool, whether it's the right tool for the moment or not. We have to be conscious of this manipulation so that students can learn when to say no to technology.
- **As I work, does it feel like this is taking too long? Do I feel frustrated with this task? Why? What's getting in my way?** Is it the content, the tools, the process? Can the student articulate a question for their teacher that gets at the root of their frustration? Is the student's attention sticking with the work or are they too distracted to get this done right now? Does the student need a break? As Beth explained in Section 2, self-monitoring during work is an essential part of becoming a strong learner. At times our learning plans need to be revised. It's OK to sometimes pause, take a break, and reconsider whether we should be using that tool to learn at that moment.

to some tools, like sentence stems, they could fall back on. It hadn't given them enough of a specific sense of where their struggle was and what they could do better. So, these kids knew how to self-evaluate, they knew their conversations were lacking, and they knew they had to do something about it. They were struggling to envision what that something was. Part of that struggle, it seemed to me, was the absence of data specific to them. If they could see what their conversation looked like from the outside, then they'd have a clearer sense of how they could improve. So I made a video of their conversation using a tablet and asked that they watch and reflect: In the video, what goes well in the conversation? What could be better? I walked away and left them to it, confident that with the right data, they'd figure things out.

When I returned to the group, they were ready with a list of things they felt they needed to work on:

- Devin does most of the talking.
- Sometimes they just say they agree but they do not explain why.
- They do not grow ideas together.
- They stare at each other.

"Choose one of these issues," I suggested, "and decide on an action plan." When they chose to work on growing ideas together, I asked them how they were going to do that. "We are going to focus on why a character says and does certain things."

Students who self-direct their learning learn how to overcome challenges and how to learn beyond superficial content. Tech in and of itself does not do the work, but rather increases options for overcoming challenges.

"And how will you keep track of that?"

"We'll create a Google Doc and list our ideas. We will each have our own color font and add our own thinking under each other's thoughts. Then we will use this to help us grow ideas and think more deeply about the characters." I let these students know the outstanding work they had done, and then I questioned, "How will you know if this plan is working?" The students responded that they intend to video themselves again in a week to see if they had improved.

In student-directed learning experiences, like book clubs, it's important that we give students a framework for examining and growing their learning. Students who self-direct their learning learn how to overcome challenges and how to learn beyond superficial content. Tech in and of itself does not do the work, but rather increases options for overcoming challenges. See Figure 3–8 for the basic template that I followed with The Book Worms.

FIGURE 3–8 *Questions to Plan Self-Directed Learning*

- What is my goal for this work?
- What's going well?
- What isn't? If uncertain, what more do I need to get a better perspective on that?
- What do I want to focus on getting better at?
- What do I need to do to improve? What can I use as a mentor to reach my goal?
- How will I keep track of how I'm doing?

This example reflects our goal in using technology: The Book Worms' decision-making was informed, not driven, by technology. We hit the sweet spot when technology promotes effortful mental activity by deepening learning and extending students' thinking beyond what they already know (Wartella 2015), as the use of Google Docs and the video recording did for The Book Worms.

Digital Reading to Build Background Knowledge

To expand beyond what they already know, learners rely on background knowledge. That push and pull of previous and new understandings requires teachers to be nimble at providing the right background knowledge at the right moment. Of course, this is a challenge because rarely do two students have the same background knowledge on a given topic, let alone an entire class. In a highly functioning literacy classroom, students access a variety of texts to build their background knowledge, and technology offers increased access to background knowledge from a variety of authentic contexts and multimedia resources. This is a habit many students have cultivated in their home tech life, consulting with YouTube, social media, and Google to get cheats to video games, new dance moves, and even cooking tips. We can tap that habit and bring it into our classrooms to apply to more academic background knowledge needs. Students know that adults do this all the time, making this particular move not only effective, but also authentic. Students can build background knowledge by more than just reading a conventional print text. They can learn information from different formats (audio, video, visual) and have those formats scaffolded (print to audio, captioned videos) to access information, experiences, and experts that are not present in our physical classroom. On the All About Birds website (TheCornellLab n.d.), students can view the bird cam as it livestreams a bird's nest throughout the egg-hatching and chick-growth processes. Viewers can collect, analyze, and report data just as ornithologists do. As historians, students can visit the National Museum of African American History and Culture (n.d.) via their digital resources to read and write about race, history, culture, and current events. There is an abundance of high-quality content.

Students can build background knowledge by more than just reading a conventional print text. They can learn information from different formats (audio, video, visual) and have those formats scaffolded (print to audio, captioned videos) to access information, experiences, and experts that are not present in our physical classroom.

Of course, reading digital texts needs to be taught! Imagine being a young learner who is still developing word recognition and comprehension skills and then finding yourself reading websites with text written at various reading levels, along with working to understand information shared through graphics, videos, and podcasts. Kids need to be explicitly taught how to comprehend the wide variety of text formats presented, and how to create a mental model of the information or story, no matter the multimedia format in which the ideas are presented (see Figure 3–9).

FIGURE 3–9 *Prompts for Understanding Multimedia Texts*

MEDIA	PROMPTS FOR UNDERSTANDING MULTIMEDIA
Print	**Before reading:** Preview the text; look over the headings to see how the information is organized. Notice any hyperlinks on the page and decide when you would like to navigate to them. **During reading:** Pause at strategic points to check your understanding while forming a mental model of the text's meaning; take notes if it's helpful. **After reading:** Synthesize the text into a few sentences that include the kernel of meaning.
Image (photo, infographic, symbol)	**Before viewing:** Identify who created and/or published the image, their credibility, and possible biases. Notice where the author decided to place the images and ask yourself why. Is there not enough text? Is it adding to the concept being discussed? Is it presenting a visual summary of the text? **During viewing:** Look over the image as a whole, then zoom in on smaller details. **After viewing:** Consider how biases may have caused information to be presented in a certain way or why information may have been left out. Synthesize the images with the text for a bigger and better understanding of the text.
Video	**Before viewing:** Identify who created and/or published the video, their credibility, and possible biases. Decide on the order in which you will read the text. Should you watch the video before or after reading the text? **During viewing:** Pause at strategic points to check your understanding while forming a mental model of the text's meaning; take notes if it's helpful. **After viewing:** Consider how biases may have caused information to be presented in a certain way or why information may have been left out. Synthesize the information in the video with the text for a bigger and better understanding.

(Continues)

(Continued)

Audio	**Before listening:** For podcasts, identify who created and/or published the podcast, their credibility, and possible biases; for audiobooks, listen to the introduction or preface to gain insights (typically gleamed from the book cover) to activate background knowledge and create anticipation. Make a thoughtful decision on when to listen to the audio. Will it be before the text or after? **During listening:** Pause periodically to check understanding and to jot down notes. **After listening:** For podcasts, consider how biases may have caused information to be presented in a certain way or why information may have been left out; for audiobooks, synthesize the text into a few sentences that include the kernel of meaning.

Curation of Multimedia Texts

From Wikipedia to Wonderopolis to National Geographic for Kids to Newsela, there are many great digital text resources for activating and building background knowledge. However, sometimes that abundance can be too much, particularly for students learning to navigate multimedia texts. When students are inundated with content, they can become so busy sorting through it that they have little, if any, time to practice critical reading skills. (And often some, but not all, digital texts on a platform are the quality we need.) Whether in the analog or digital world, much of a teacher's job is content curation. This curation work becomes exponentially more crucial in the digital realm. When students are taking their first forays into multimedia texts, it can be extremely helpful for students if teachers sift through the most accessible options for their students and scaffold students through their teacher-selected collections. Once students develop media literacy skills, they can begin to recommend resources to add to the classroom collection (see Figure 3-10).

Whether in the analog or digital world, much of a teacher's job is content curation.

FIGURE 3–10 *Further Resources on Media Literacy*

- **The Be Internet Awesome program (Google, n.d.) shares with families and educators activities for developing media literacy skills through a fun, interactive game approach.** https://beinternetawesome.withgoogle.com/
- **Common Sense Media (Common Sense Education, n.d.) has developed a digital citizenship curriculum for K–12, where a teacher can lead students through activities for developing a sense of how to stay safe and communicate effectively with others on the Internet.** https://www.commonsense.org/education/digital-citizenship
- **Media Education Lab (Media Education Lab, n.d.) presents lesson plans, videos, and teaching resources for integrating media literacy into instruction.** https://mediaeducationlab.com/curriculum/materials

A curated virtual classroom library can be a helpful source of knowledge-building resources, whether students are learning in the school classroom or remotely (see Figure 3–11). Multimedia texts may include e-books, audio books, articles, blog posts, tutorial videos, images, and podcasts. Just as with physical books, digital texts can be organized around themes and topics, with links placed on a document or an online learning space for easy access.

Researching Online

Asking students to use the web to research a question or a topic may seem relatively simple on the surface—after all, millions of people look up information using internet searches every day—especially after so many students leaned heavily on internet searches during the pandemic; how hard can it be? Searching is easy, but finding information that is credible, understanding this information, and synthesizing it into the small chunk needed for a project, without plagiarizing, is not so easy. Students need an internalized process of evaluating text reliability to protect themselves

FIGURE 3–11 *Making Curation Decisions for Background Knowledge*

QUESTIONS TO ASK WHEN CURATING	HOW IT COULD LOOK
What content do I want my students to be able to access?	American Revolution
Are there particular organizations, people, or information that is crucial to their understanding that I need to include in the text sets?	▶ New York Historical Society ▶ The Smithsonian ▶ People belonging to groups that have been marginalized: Indigenous peoples, Black people, and all other people of color; women; members of the working class ▶ The perspectives of key cities such as Philadelphia, Boston, and New York
What type of media am I including? Am I providing a variety of modalities?	▶ Short documentary video ▶ Playlist of music from the time period ▶ Primary documents with translation/commentary available digitally ▶ Articles written for students ▶ E-books ▶ Photos of historical places and items ▶ Artwork contemporary to the era
In what ways is this content made accessible? Language translation? Written form? Audio? Something else?	▶ Translation extension for articles ▶ Videos that have the option of closed caption in home language ▶ E-books that have either a read-to-me feature or that can also be found in audio book form

QUESTIONS TO ASK WHEN CURATING	HOW IT COULD LOOK
What themes or subtopics might you include?	▶ Causes of the war ▶ Unsung heroes ▶ Geography ▶ Allies ▶ Role of children ▶ Key events
What are the criteria for each subtopic text set? How many texts will be available? What is the readability range? What voices or perspectives will be included in each set?	Each subtopic text set must have: ▶ 5–7 texts ▶ Readability levels second to sixth grade ▶ BIPOC voices

against the mistakes (purposeful or inadvertent), misunderstandings, and bias found in texts (see Figure 3–12 for an example). We want students to become adept at finding their own information, but we also have to respect how overwhelming this can be. When we were students, a librarian or teacher selected texts, which were first vetted by the author and editor before making their way to our school and classroom library. With the vastness of the internet at their fingertips, our students are locating, reading, and evaluating texts, some of which have few, if any, filters between the author and the reader. They are also coming across texts created with blatant bias or an intent to make money or unduly influence behavior. Being an effective and efficient web reader takes students who can think critically. Are we teaching our students to be information literate? If so, are we starting early enough?

As Beth described in Section 2, studies show that media literacy skills not only help students identify bias and misinformation, but also help support them develop critical literacy skills across media.

FIGURE 3–12 *Questions for Evaluating a Website as an Information Source*

THE 5 W'S OF WEBSITE EVALUATION

Who?

- Who wrote the pages, and are they an expert?
- Is a biography of the author included?
- How can I find out more about the author?

What?

- What does the author say is the purpose of the site?
- What else might the author have in mind for the site?
- What makes the site easy to use?
- What information is included, and does this information differ from other sites?

When?

- When was the site created?
- When was the site last updated?

Where?

- Where does the information come from?
- Where can I look to find out more about the sponsor of the site?

Why?

- Why is this information useful for my purpose?
- Why should I use this information?
- Why is this page better than another?

Recently, I (Beth) partnered with a second-grade teacher, Joy McGaffrey, to teach a research unit on animals from extreme environments. Although the students had all used internet searches many times, both in and out of school, this unit was their first with academic research, so we scaffolded their experience by using a student-friendly internet search engine. Kiddle, the example we used in this study, is a visual search engine for kids. With Kiddle, search results are filtered, adding an extra layer to the school district's firewalls and protecting the students from seeing inappropriate websites or images during their search. We also provided students with a note-taking guide that students handwrote notes in to avoid cutting and pasting content. See Figure 3–13 for one student's completed note-taking guide and published piece.

FIGURE 3–13a and 13b *Brea's Note-Taking Guide and Published Piece*

(a)

Looking for Information Name: Brea

My animal is a Penguins and lives in the Artiac.

How tall is the animal?	Where did I find the information?
4 feet tall	Penguins Chicks by Betty Tatham
How much does the animal weigh?	**Where did I find the information?**
40 Pounds	Penguin Chicks by Betty Tatham
Describe how the animal looks	**Where did I find the information?**
chicks are soft and gray	Penguin Chicks by Betty Tathmam
Explain how the animal moves	**Where did I find the information?**
thay Dive 1,500 feet in the oeacn	Kids Britannica website
Describe where the animal lives	**Where did I find the information?**
icy, cold and Blow zero Anartica	Active wild.com
Name three things the animal eats	**Where did I find the information?**
Fish Squid Krill	Activewild.com

(b)

Penguins

Penguins are 4 feet tall and weigh 40 pounds. The chicks are soft and gray and cute! They dive in the ocean to 1,500 feet. It is icy, cold and below zero in the Antarctica where they live. Penguins eat fish, squid, krill.

Digital Tools That Enhance Metacognition

Technology, especially connected to inquiry, can facilitate the collecting and sharing of reflections and add a motivational element that can keep reflection engaging for students.

Digital content can look "expert," so teaching metacognition around technology becomes essential. Reflection can occur with or without technology, but, often, because of the efficiency of the tools and the ease of making and sharing a professional-looking product, reflection can get short shrift. The good news is that, as was discussed in Section 2, technology, especially connected to inquiry, can facilitate the collecting and sharing of reflections and add a motivational element that can keep reflection engaging for students. During Maria Salvator's sixth-grade social studies class, students research events from the past that shape our lives today. Once a week, during this three-week project-based learning activity, students are asked to reflect by answering three questions:

1. What have I learned?
2. How did I learn it?
3. What am I ready to learn next?

The more teachers and peers model metacognition, the more students can learn to deepen their learning by intentional metacognition, normalize struggle as part of learning, and expand their repertoire of problem-solving strategies by seeing how others overcome struggle.

By identifying *how* they learned, students often get to the heart of *what* they learned. Classmates, teachers, and families can view the reflections and add their own reflection. In this way we build a visible chain of reflection that shows students their thinking is valuable and that it can grow.

Creating a meaningful reflection takes explicit instruction, modeling, practice, and a safe learning space where students know it's OK to say, "I didn't do that well" or "I am not sure how to do that" and also won't be judged for saying, "I am good at this." Sharing an inner dialogue aloud makes struggles and successes visible and audible. Through this personal feedback loop, students bring to light information about their performance that can be used to deepen learning and make adaptations for their future learning. The more teachers and peers model metacognition, the more students can learn to deepen their learning by intentional metacognition, normalize struggle as part of learning, and expand their repertoire of problem-solving strategies by seeing how others overcome struggle. See Figure 3–14 for technology tools that support metacognition.

This kind of metacognition helps us learn not only that our students completed an assignment, but also the thinking process that makes them writers and readers.

FIGURE 3–14 *Technology Resources That Support Metacognition*

TOOL AND PURPOSE	QUESTIONS TO GUIDE METACOGNITION
Screen capture (e.g., Screencast-o-matic) for reflecting on the writing and creating process	▶ What is my decision-making process in creating this piece? ▶ Why did I make those choices? ▶ How did those choices address my audience's needs?
Digital portfolios (e.g., Seesaw, a digital portfolio platform) for displaying illustrations, images, screenshots, and videos	▶ How does what I created show what I learned? ▶ What am I most proud of in my piece of work? Why? ▶ What turned out differently than I expected in this piece of work? Why?
Virtual bulletin boards (e.g., Padlet or Jamboard) for tracking, sharing and growing ideas	▶ What part of the text feels significant and worth further evaluating? ▶ How did I get to my new idea or theory? ▶ What else can I say about what you shared and how it connects to what I shared?
Concept mapping (e.g., Bubbl.us or MindMeister) for sorting information and making connections and seeing relationships across content	▶ What is the central idea or concept here? ▶ What are some subtopics I can see for this topic? Is there a way to group the information in a different way? ▶ By looking across the way the information is laid out, what connections am I seeing? What surprises me?

Digital Collaboration

During the pandemic, we were reminded of how much peer collaboration is essential to student learning. Many students' engagement faltered without connection to their peers. With technology, we've often seen that students collaborate better. Technology allows us to pause and consider our feedback without the awkward silences we might have face-to-face.

When we plan for group projects, small groups, centers, seminars, or partner work, we can build in more ways for our kids to learn from each other and we can learn by observing their collaboration. In our experience, the students who are reluctant to contribute in class seem to find more voice and confidence when contributing in a digital way. See Figure 3–15 to assess for when tech collaboration is effective.

FIGURE 3–15 *How to Assess Effective Collaboration Using Technology*

Technology fosters collaboration when . . .

- Learners are co-engaged, or work together on one device, rather than one student working and one student just watching.
- Two or more students create a project simultaneously within a shared document or collaborative digital project site or app.
- A back-and-forth discussion of ideas occurs through typing, video conferencing, or recording feedback to share with others and invite a similar response (e.g., Flipgrid).
- Learners can communicate with experts, classmates away from school (e.g., long-term illness, traveling, snow day), or students at other schools via email, online chat, or video conference.

Collaboration with Shared Drives

Collaboration can be organized through shared drives such as Google Classroom, Microsoft Teams, or school-based shared drives. All shared drives offer certain characteristics (communication tools, work collaboration possibilities, various platforms, apps, and extensions that can be stored and accessed easily). A shared drive creates opportunities for students to provide feedback, build on each other's thinking, and take inspiration from one another's work. For example, if a student feels that a piece they've written is super powerful, we can encourage them to put it into our shared mentor folder. Others students can peek in and be inspired by ideas as they would any mentor text. See Figure 3–16 for some guidelines for collaborating with shared drives.

A shared drive creates opportunities for students to provide feedback, build on each other's thinking, and take inspiration from one another's work.

FIGURE 3–16 *Guidelines for Collaborating with Shared Drives*

A good collaboration platform is one that

- allows all members equal access to participation
- is well organized and meaningful to all
- includes directions and a guide
- allows students to take agency over their research
- gives access to teacher for review and feedback

Students might use shared drives to

- collaborate in book clubs or research groups to organize ideas
- assign homework to each other
- create projects and work on them outside of school.

Figure 3–17 shows an example of a fifth-grade reading group, The Shooting Stars, working in a shared drive to gather their thinking on craft moves in the short film *Kitbull.*

FIGURE 3–17 *Reading Group Analysis of Craft Moves in Shared Drive*

The Shooting Stars

- **Introduced the character and show us how he is alone**
- Puppy is growling because he is scared
- Thinking why the dog got his attitude because of the owner treating the dog.
- The cat is building a mood and building empathy the cat is scared
- The cat is starting to feel bad for the dog because it's on a chain.
- **The cat is starting to become friends with the dog.**
- The cat scratched the dog because she thought that the dog was about to harm her. But the dog just wanted to help her.

Annotation of Digital Texts and Student Writing

One beneficial aspect of digital texts is the ability for the reader to highlight and annotate a text, any text, in a variety of ways, and then have the capability to clear off all the markings and try it again. This capability supports the reader's deeper thinking about the text. For practical purposes, choose a platform that aligns well with the devices your students can access, as well as your budget (see Figure 3–18).

FIGURE 3–18 *Guidelines for Choosing Digital Annotation Tools*

ANNOTATION CAPABILITIES	GOOD FOR	PLATFORMS OR APPS TO CONSIDER
▶ Highlighting ▶ Marginal comments ▶ Converting documents to pdfs	▶ iOS devices ▶ Windows ▶ Chromebooks ▶ Budget conscious ▶ New tech users	▶ Adobe Acrobat Reader ▶ Foxit ▶ Xodo

ANNOTATION CAPABILITIES	GOOD FOR	PLATFORMS OR APPS TO CONSIDER
▶ Long-form note-taking, embedding text into notes ▶ Embedding images, voice, and video ▶ Highlighting ▶ Marginal comments ▶ Converting documents to pdfs	▶ iOS devices ▶ Windows ▶ Chromebooks ▶ Free to moderate budgets ▶ Some experience with tech helpful	▶ Google Keep ▶ Notability ▶ Evernote
▶ Using OCR (optical character recognition) or other technology, reads aloud text when needed ▶ Translating text when needed ▶ Highlighting ▶ Marginal comments ▶ Converting documents to pdfs	▶ iOS devices ▶ Windows ▶ Chromebooks ▶ Free to moderate budgets ▶ Students who would benefit from support in reading text	▶ Snap&Read ▶ Texthelp's Read&Write

One powerful form of virtual feedback you and your students might find beneficial is to highlight and annotate a mentor text as part of your writing instruction. For example, you can select a portion of a student's writing that could use revision and send them an excerpt of familiar mentor text, inviting them to "try it this way." You might even consider gathering different mentor text pieces and organizing them into virtual folders or posting them on a virtual bulletin board, then jotting or recording quick ways for kids to try these out. Likewise, students can create virtual writing journals of excerpts of other people's writing they admire.

Digital Publishing

We know writing is so much more than simply getting words down on the page—it's about exploring ideas, structuring them, and crafting them. Just as in other art forms, the tools we use have a direct impact on the products we create. For writers who struggle, simply using a word processor instead of pen and paper can make a noticeable difference in the students' writing.

For the research on how word processing helps improve writing quality, see Section 2, page 29.

When we ask ourselves what we want our kids to produce to show their understanding, we can also consider what digital tools are available that allow for student creation to be enhanced. What might students be able to do with technology that is important to this objective and cannot be done without it? At the end of a writing unit, we judge students' mastery by their ability to produce a piece of work that addresses the unit's content. Traditionally, all their work is in one of two formats: handwritten or typed. In limiting our kids to only these media for writing, we are limiting their choice and voice. As adult writers, we consider where to put diagrams, pictures, charts, and other information on a page to get our ideas across to the reader. We consider not only the best *way* to present the information but also the best *outlet* to present their information. The same should be true for our students. If our objective is to see how well students can produce something that is truly their own, then it is imperative that we let them have a choice in the outlet of these ideas. Students might decide to create a digital book, they might decide to create an infographic, or they might even decide to create a video with a narrative. We can learn so much from our kids about what they can do when we give them ways to express their thoughts, using twenty-first-century technology.

Asking them which tools best work for their purpose assesses the transfer of their learning in a deep way. I give my students a choice of how they want to deliver their information (paper and pen, digital book, infographic, a comic app, Google Slides, or Google Docs). See Figure 3–19 for options for publishing with technology.

FIGURE 3–19 *Options for Digital Publishing*

TOOL	MAY WORK ESPECIALLY WELL FOR
Book editor (e.g., Book Creator, Kindle Kids' Book Creator)	▶ Ease-of-use in creating a book ▶ Choice of page design
Infographics (e.g., Infogram, Adobe Spark, Canva)	▶ Presenting big ideas ▶ Synthesis of images and text ▶ Thoughtful decisions around font choice and placement of text and images
Comic app (e.g., Comic Life, Toontastic, Make Beliefs Comix)	▶ Publishing comic books
Slides (e.g., Google Slides, PowerPoint, Nearpod)	▶ Group or individual presentations ▶ Collaboration among students
Word Processing with collaboration or share features (e.g., Google Docs, Co:Writer, Microsoft Word)	▶ Quick feedback through comments ▶ Rough drafts and editing ▶ Collaboration among students ▶ Choice of placement of text, images, and hyperlinks
Creating a Movie (e.g., iMovie, Microsoft Movie Maker)	▶ Students showing not telling what they are publishing ▶ Lots of creativity beyond text ▶ Synthesis of setting, plot and artifacts
Screen Capture with Voice Over (e.g., Screencast-O-Matic, Screencastify, ShowMe)	▶ Diving deeper into author's craft ▶ Teaching the published materials to others

Outside of considering a range of ways to publish finished writing pieces for writing's sake, students can also create finished products where the goal is to teach. Postpandemic, most of us, as well as our students, are very familiar with flipped lessons, sometimes called asynchronous teaching. Those lessons are prerecorded, so the content is front-loaded and class time or one-on-one time is used to practice the work. See Figure 3–20 for some guidelines to share with students on creating flipped lessons.

FIGURE 3–20 *Qualities of a Good Flipped Lesson*

Qualities of a Good Flipped Lesson

- Is easily accessible for all students to view
- Has transferable skills that can be revisited when needed
- Shows images and has a voice-over or video of the speaker
- Is brief (5–8 minutes)
- Has an anchor chart that can be used in the classroom
- Gives solid examples of a skill or strategy

In Suzanne's classroom, students have created flipped lessons on diverse topics like how to write a killer action scene, how to make your thinking about reading visible, how to design an awesome PowerPoint. One of the positive outcomes of using flipped lessons is that they can create more time for student collaboration during class time. As a publishing option, students deepen their learning and have fun creating flipped lessons for each other. The flipped lessons students create can be shared on a common drive or classroom shared site. Flipped lessons can be an incredibly powerful form of assessment. By watching students' flipped lessons, teachers can get a better handle on the depth of student understanding and their application of that knowledge, and even see what teaching methods they find useful.

Flipped lessons can be an incredibly powerful form of assessment.

Monitoring for Engagement and Purpose

We know what the potential of technology is, but context is always key. Just because a certain digital tool has worked with students in the past doesn't mean that tool should be used by every student moving forward. Monitoring digital tech use for engagement and purpose is essential, not just by teachers of students but by students of themselves. We want mindful, not mindless, engagement with tech. When you invite students to monitor for engagement, you open up the larger question of purposeful work. This means that students may question the work you assign. There's no doubt that this can be uncomfortable at times, but it's a good question you should be able to answer.

One of my early teaching/learning experiences came from a student who told me the group PowerPoint presentation activity I (Suzanne) had assigned was stupid. His questioning made me realize that I hadn't thought deeply enough about the one-size-fits-all publishing option I was offering students. Because he and I took the time to discuss what wasn't working, I was able to revise and expand students' options, using their input. Students saw that their voices mattered, and engagement in that project was phenomenal. Many students, including the one who challenged me, produced their best work thus far in the year. Sure, this meant that students often asked me "Why?" when I suggested possibilities, but it also meant that my teaching became about more than the limitations of my own imagination. Opening up this dialogue means that we hold ourselves more accountable to create purposeful learning experiences and improve the integrity of our teaching. Most importantly, it helps students realize they have agency in their learning. If they're not engaged, it's not because they aren't smart, but because they need to collaborate with the teacher on a better way into the learning. Creating a conversation with students about how, why, when, and whether we should use technology in learning keeps students at the center of our teaching.

Creating a conversation with students about how, why, when, and whether we should use technology in learning keeps students at the center of our teaching.

AFTERWORD

M. Colleen Cruz

Back in the last century, when I was a new teacher, I taught in a public school that had a computer lab. It was run by an absolutely brilliant educator, Mary Sue Lindley, who taught computer classes to all students and also supported teachers who were interested in bringing more tech into their teaching. At the time, the bringing of tech into teaching was a very hard sell for a lot of us. Personal computers were still not in every home, even if they were becoming more common. The internet was still accessed with dial-up modems.

One day, while I was hanging out in the computer lab after school, checking my email because I didn't have a computer at home, Mary Sue asked if I would be willing to pilot some technology with my students in writing. She showed me this round, turquoise machine, an Alpha Smart—part word processor, part sort of computer. Although I was a bit leery, I have also always been invigorated by new ideas, and I jumped at the chance to be a pilot teacher. What I did next was embarrassingly *meh*. A few students stumbled through trying to draft using the machines. I stumbled around, trying to figure out how to make the things something more worthwhile than a typewriter. And ultimately the machines ended up being another newfangled thing that did nothing to improve student learning. If anything, those turquoise machines became another obstacle students had to overcome on their way to learning. As my years in the classroom added up, technology vastly changed and improved, but I continued to treat it as something more akin to an add-on or extra, with little instruction in actual ways to merge literacy with technology. I thought very little about how to authentically integrate technology into my teaching, allowing its capabilities and my attention span to determine how it was utilized.

What I would have given (and my students, quite frankly) for me to have read the book you have just finished! What a difference it would have made to have been introduced to the revolutionary idea that technology is not some magical thing that I have no control of, but rather a tool that can and should be used to meet the needs of both teacher and student.

With constant upgrades, innovations, and new capabilities, the technology coming at teachers (and expected to be instantly integrated into the classroom) has never been more overwhelming. Elizabeth Dobler and Suzanne Kelly have managed to cut through all the noise and focus on what matters most—teaching students, not technology. By naming the technology temptations teachers face (It's engaging! It's responsive! It can differentiate automatically!) and how easy it is to get lost in the abundance of options and steadily increasing administrative demands, Beth and Suzanne have put their arms around our shoulders like old friends, encouraging us to put all of that aside. Beth and Suzanne offer us a different path, one where we are the ones in charge of the technology and can use what we know from research and powerful teaching methods to move forward with intention, making technology be our assistant in creating powerfully literate students and citizens.

REFERENCES

Alberta Learning. 2004. "Focus on Inquiry: A Teacher's Guide to Implementing Inquiry Based Learning." Edmonton, Alberta: Alberta Learning. https://open.alberta.ca/publications/0778526666.

Almasi, Janice F. 1995. "The Nature of Fourth Graders' Sociocognitive Conflicts in Peer-Led and Teacher-Led Discussions of Literature." *Reading Research Quarterly* 30 (3): 314–51.

Antonio, Dee, and Guthrie, John T. 2008. "Reading Is Social: Bringing Peer Interaction to the Text." In *Engaging Adolescents in Reading*, edited by John T. Guthrie, 49–63. Thousand Oaks, CA: Corwin.

Aragon, Cecilia R., Sarah S. Poon, Andrés Monroy-Hernández, and Diana Aragon. 2009. "A Tale of Two Online Communities: Fostering Collaboration and Creativity in Scientists and Children." In *Proceedings of the Seventh ACM Conference on Creativity and Cognition: C&C '09*, 9–18. New York: Association for Computing Machinery.

Barab, Sasha A., James G. MaKinster, Julie A. Moore, and Donald J. Cunningham. 2001. "Designing and Building an On-Line Community: The Struggle to Support Sociability in the Inquiry Learning Forum." *Educational Technology Research and Development* 49 (4): 71–96.

Block, Meghan K., and Stephanie L. Strachan. 2019. "The Impact of External Audience on Second Graders' Writing Quality." *Reading Horizons: A Journal of Literacy and Language Arts* 58 (2). https://scholarworks.wmich.edu/reading_horizons/vol58/iss2/5.

Boyle, Elizabeth A., Thomas A. Hainey, Thomas M. Connolly, Grant Gray, Jeffrey Earp, Michela Ott, Theodore Lim, Manuel Ninaus, Claudia Ribeiro, and Joãn Pereira. 2016. "An Update to the Systematic Literature Review of Empirical Evidence of the Impacts and Outcomes of Computer Games and Serious Games." *Computers & Education,* 94: 178–92.

Bridge, Corbin. n.d. "The Education Technology (EdTech) Industry: Overview of Mergers, Acquisitions and Venture Capital Trends & Investments." Investment Bank. https://investmentbank.com/edtech-industry/.

Bruner, Jerome. 1960. *The Process of Education.* Cambridge, MA: Harvard University Press.

Buckner, Elizabeth, and Paul Kim. 2014. "Integrating Technology and Pedagogy for Inquiry Based Learning: The Stanford Mobile Inquiry-Based Learning Environment (SMILE)." *Prospects: Quarterly Review of Comparative Education* 44 (1): 99–118.

Chang, Hsin-Yi, Chris Quintana, and Joseph S. Krajcik. 2010. "The Impact of Designing and Evaluating Molecular Animations on How Well Middle School Students Understand the Particulate Nature of Matter." *Science Education* 94 (1): 73–94.

Chen, Chang-Huan, and Yong-Chi Yang. 2019. "Revisiting the Effects of Project-Based Learning on Students' Academic Achievement: A Meta-Analysis Investigating Moderators." *Educational Research Review* 26: 71–81.

Cheung, Alan, and Robert E. Slavin. 2011. *The Effectiveness of Education Technology for Enhancing Reading Achievement: A Meta-Analysis*. Center for Research and Reform in Education. Baltimore, MD: Johns Hopkins University.

Coiro, Julie. 2017. "Advancing Reading Engagement and Achievement Through Personal Digital Inquiry, Critical Literacy, and Skillful Argumentation." In *Improving Reading and Reading Engagement in the 21st Century*, edited by Clarence Ng and Brenden Bartlett, 49–76. Singapore: Springer.

Coiro, Julie, Diane Carver Sekeres, Jill Castek, and Lizabeth A. Guzniczak. 2014. "Comparing 3rd, 4th, and 5th Graders' Collaborative Interactions While Engaged in Online Inquiry." *Journal of Education* 194 (2): 1–16.

Colella, V. 2000. "Participatory Simulations: Building Collaborative Understanding Through Immersive Dynamic Modeling." *Journal of Learning Sciences* 9 (4): 471–500.

Common Sense Education. n.d. "Everything You Need to Teach Digital Citizenship." https://www.commonsense.org/education/digital-citizenship.

Goodyear, Peter, and Symeon Retalis. 2010. *Technology-Enhanced Learning: Design Patterns and Pattern Language.* Rotterdam, The Netherlands: Sense Publishers.

Google. n.d. "Be Internet Awesome." https://beinternetawesome.withgoogle.com/en_us.

Graham, Steve, and Dolores Perin. 2007. *Writing Next: Effective Strategies to Improve Writing of Adolescents in Middle and High School.* New York: Carnegie Corporation.

Hacker, Douglas J., John Dunlosky, and Arthur C. Graesser. 2009. "A Growing Sense of 'Agency.'" In *The Handbook of Metacognition in Education*, edited by Douglas J. Hacker, John Dunlosky, and Arthur C. Graesser, 1–4. New York: Routledge.

Hall, Tracey E., Nicole Cohen, Ge Vue, and Patricia Ganley. 2015. "Addressing Learning Disabilities with UDL and Technology: Strategic Reader." *Learning Disability Quarterly* 38 (2): 72–83.

Hayes, John Richard, and Linda Flower. 1980. "Identifying the Organization of Writing Processes." In *Cognitive Processes in Writing*, edited by Lee W. Gregg and Erwin R. Steinberg, 3–30. Hillsdale, NJ: Lawrence Erlbaum Associates.

Hirsh-Pasek, Kathy, Jennifer M. Zosh, Roberta Michnick, Golinkoff, James H. Gray, Michael B. Robb, and Jordy Kaufman. 2015. "Putting Education in 'Educational' Apps: Lessons from the Science of Learning." *Psychological Science in the Public Interest* 16 (1): 3–34.

Hobbs, Renee. 2017. "Teaching and Learning in a Post-Truth World." *Educational Leadership* 75 (3): 26–31. http://www.ascd.org/publications/educational_leadership/nov17/vol75/num03/Teaching_and_Learning_in_a_Post-Truth_World.aspx.

Hobbs, Renee, and David Cooper Moore. 2013. *Discovering Media Literacy: Digital Media and Popular Culture in Elementary School.* Thousand Oaks CA: Corwin/Sage.

Hutchison, A., Beth Beschorner, and Denise A. Schmidt-Crawford. 2012. "Exploring the Use of the iPad for Literacy Learning." *The Reading Teacher* 66 (1): 15–23.

Hutchison, Amy C., and Jamie Colwell. 2014. "The Potential of Digital Technologies to Support Literacy Instruction Relevant to the Common Core State Standards." *Journal of Adolescent & Adult Literacy* 58 (2): 147–56.

Hutchison, Amy C., and David Reinking. 2011. "Teachers' Perceptions of Integrating Information and Communications Technologies

Common Sense Media. n.d. "Educational Apps That Don't Need Wi-Fi or Data." https://www.commonsensemedia.org/lists/educational-apps-that-dont-need-wi-fi-or-data.

Conradi, Kristin. 2014. "Tapping Technology's Potential to Motivate Readers." *Kappan* 96 (3): 54–57. doi: 10.1177/0031721714557454.

TheCornellLab n.d. "Red-Tailed Hawks." All About Birds. https://www.allaboutbirds.org/cams/red-tailed-hawks/.

Coyne, Peggy, Bart Pisha, Bridget Dalton, Lucille Zeph, and Nancy Cook Smith. 2012. "Literacy by Design: A Universal Design for Learning Approach for Students with Significant Intellectual Disabilities." *Remedial and Special Education* 31 (4).

Dalton, Bridget. 2012. "Multimodal Composition and the Common Core State Standards." *The Reading Teacher* 66 (4): 333–39.

Darling-Hammond, Linda, Molly B. Zielezinksi, and Shelley Goldman. 2014. "Using Technology to Support At-Risk Students' Learning." SCOPE. https://edpolicy.stanford.edu/sites/default/files/scope-pub-using-technology-report.pdf.

Fazlullah, Amina. 2020. "Help Students and Their Families Access Low-Cost and Free Internet, Devices, and Internet Content. Common Sense Education." Common Sense Media. https://www.commonsense.org/education/articles/5-ways-to-get-all-students-connected-for-distance-learning.

Federal Communications Commission. 2019. *Inquiry Concerning Deployment of Advanced Telecommunications Capability to All Americans in a Reasonable and Timely Fashion*. Washington, DC: Federal Communications Commission. https://www.fcc.gov/document/broadband-deployment-report-digital-divide-narrowing-substantially-0.

Furtak, Erin M., Tina Seidel, H. Iverson, and Derek C. Briggs. 2012. "Experimental and Quasi-Experimental Studies of Inquiry-Based Science Teaching: A Meta-Analysis." *Review of Educational Research* 82 (3): 300–29.

Gee, James Paul. 2003. *What Video Games Have to Teach Us About Learning and Literacy*. New York: Palgrave/Macmillan.

Goldberg, Amie, Michael Russell, and Abigail Cook. 2003. "The Effect of Computers on Student Writing: A Meta-Analysis of Studies from 1992 to 2002." *The Journal of Technology, Learning, and Assessment* 2 (1). https://ejournals.bc.edu/index.php/jtla/article/view/1661.

for Citizenship. https://eavi.eu/beyond-fake-news-10-types-misleading-info/.

Vygotsky, Lev S. 1986. *Thought and Language*. Translated by A. Kozulin. Cambridge, MA: MIT Press.

Wartella, Ellen. 2015. "Education Apps: What We Do and Do Not Know." *Psychological Science in the Public Interest* 16 (1): 1-2.

Webb, Theresa, and Kathryn Martin. 2012. "Evaluation of a US School-Based Media Literacy Violence Prevention Curriculum on Changes in Knowledge and Critical Thinking Among Adolescents." *Journal of Children and Media* 6 (4): 430–49.

Weil, Leonora G., Stephen M. Fleming, Iroise Dumontheil, Emma J. Kilford, Rimona S. Weil, Geraint Rees, Raymond J. Dolan, and Sarah Blakemore. 2013. "The Development of Metacognitive Ability in Adolescents." *Consciousness & Cognition* 22 (1): 264–71.

Williams, Cheri, and Sandra Beam. 2019. "Technology and Writing: Review of Research." *Computers & Education* 128: 227–42.

Wouters, Pieter, Christof van Nimwegen, Herre van Oostendorp, and Erik D. van der Spek. 2013. "A Meta-Analysis of the Cognitive and Motivational Effects of Serious Games." *Journal of Educational Psychology* 105 (2): 249–65.

Wu, Xiaoying, Richard C. Anderson, Kim T. Nguyen-Jahiel, and Brian W. Miller. 2013."Enhancing Motivation and Engagement Through Collaborative Discussion." *Journal of Educational Psychology* 105 (3): 622–32.

Yang, Fan-Ying, Ming-Jung Tsai, Gou-Li Chiou, Sylvia Wen-Yu Lee, Cheng-Chieh Chang, and Li-Ling Chen. 2018. "Instructional Suggestions Supporting Science Learning in Digital Environments Based on a Review of Eye Tracking Studies." *Educational Technology & Society* 21 (2): 28–45.

Yang, Xinyuan, Li-Jen Kuo, Xeujun Ji, and Erin McTigue. 2018. "A Critical Examination of the Relationship Among Research, Theory, and Practice: Technology and Reading Instruction." *Computers & Education* 125: 62–73.

Yehudit, Judy Dori, Shirly Avargil, Zehavit Kohen, and Liora Saar. 2018. "Context-Based Learning and Metacognitive Prompts for Enhancing Scientific Text Comprehension." *International Journal of Science Education* 40 (10): 1119–20.

Okojie, Mabel CPO, Anthony A. Olinzock, and Tinukwa C. Okojie-Boulder.
2006. "The Pedagogy of Technology Integration." *Journal of Technology Studies* 32 (2): 66–71.

Paris, Scott G., Barbara A.Wasik, and Julianne C. Turner. 1991. "The Development of Strategic Readers." In *Handbook of Reading Research* vol. 2, edited by Rebecca Barr, Michael L. Kamil, Peter Mosenthal, and P. David Pearson, 609–40. White Plains, NY: Longman.

Pew Research Center. 2019. "Internet/Broadband Fact Sheet." https://www.pewresearch.org/internet/fact-sheet/internet-broadband/#who-has-home-broadband.

Piaget, Jean. 1972. *To Understand Is to Invent.* New York: Viking.

Picton, Irene, Christina Clark, and Tim Judge. 2020. "Video Game Playing and Literacy: A Survey of Young People Aged 11 to 16." National Literacy Trust. https://cdn.literacytrust.org.uk/media/documents/Video_game_playing_and_literacy_report_final_updated.pdf.

Proctor, C. Patrick, Bridget Dalton, and Dana L. Grisham. 2007. "Scaffolding English Language Learners and Struggling Readers in a Universal Literacy Environment with Embedded Strategy Instruction and Vocabulary Support." *Journal of Literacy Research* 39 (1): 71–93.

Proctor, Michael D., and Yaela Marks. 2013. "A Survey of Exemplar Teacher's Perceptions, Use, and Access of Computer-Based Games and Technology for Classroom Instruction." *Computers & Education* 62: 172–80.

Purcell, Kristen, Judy Buchanan, and Linda Friedrich. 2013. "The Impact of Digital Tools on Student Writing and How Writing is Taught in Schools." PEW Internet & American Life Project. https://www.pewinternet.org/2013/07/16/the-impact-of-digital-tools-on-student-writing-and-how-writing-is-taught-in-schools/.

Rose, David H., and Anne Meyer. 2002. *Teaching Every Student in the Digital Age: Universal Design for Learning*. Alexandria, VA: Association for Supervision & Curriculum Development.

Saavedra, Anna R., and V. Darleen Opfer. 2012. "Learning 21st Century Skills Requires 21st Century Teaching." *Phi Delta Kappan* 94 (2): 8–13.

Steinberg, Luc. 2017. "Infographic: Beyond Fake News—10 Types of Misleading News—Seventeen Languages." Media Literacy

Research, edited by Charles A. MacArthur, Steven Graham, and Jill Fitzgerald, 248–61. New York: Guilford.

Mayer, Richard E., and Roxana Moreno. 1998. "A Split-Attention Effect in Multimedia Learning: Evidence for Dual Processing Systems in Working Memory." *Journal of Educational Psychology 90* (2): 312–20.

McDermott, Peter, and Kathleen A. Gormley. 2015. "Teachers' Use of Technology in Elementary Reading Lessons." *Reading Psychology* 37: 121–46.

McDonald, Scott, and Nancy Butler Songer. 2008. "Enacting Classroom Inquiry: Theorizing Teachers' Conceptions of Science Teaching." *Science Education* 92 (6): 973–93.

McLaughlin, Clare. 2016. "The Homework Gap: The 'Cruelest Part of the Digital Divide.'" National Education Association. https://www.nea.org/advocating-for-change/new-from-nea/homework-gap-cruelest-part-digital-divide.

Media Education Lab. n.d. "Teaching Resources." https://mediaeducationlab.com/curriculum/materials.

Mills, Kathy A., and Beryl Exley. 2014. "Time, Space, and Text in the Elementary School Digital Writing Classroom." *Written Communication* 31 (4): 434–69.

Mishra, Punya, and Matthew J. Koehler. 2006. "Technological Pedagogical Content Knowledge: A Framework for Integrating Technology in Teacher Knowledge." *Teachers College Record* 108 (6): 1017–54.

Morphy, Paul, and Steve Graham. 2012. "Word Processing Programs and Weaker Writers/Readers: A Meta-Analysis of Research Findings." *Reading & Writing* 25 (3): 641–78.

National Association of Media Literacy Education. (n.d.) "What is Media Literacy?" Center for Media Literacy. http://www.medialit.org/reading-room/what-media-literacy-namles-short-answer-and-longer-thought

National Governors Association and Council of Chief School Officers. 2010. *Common Core State Standards*. National Governors Association, Washington, DC. http://www.corestandards.org/.

National Museum of African American History and Culture. n.d. "NMAAHC Digital Resource Guide." Smithsonian. https://nmaahc.si.edu/explore/nmaahc-digital-resources-guide.

Network for Good. n.d. "Bridging the Digital Divide." https://www.networkforgood.org/topics/education/digitaldivide/.

into Literacy Instruction. A National Survey in the United States." *Reading Research Quarterly* 46 (4): 308–29.

Hutchison, Amy, and Lindsay Woodward. 2014. "A Planning Cycle for Integrating Technology into Literacy Instruction." *The Reading Teacher* 67 (6): 455–64.

Hutchison, Amy C., Lindsay Woodward, and Jamie Colwell. 2016. "What Are Preadolescent Readers Doing Online? An Examination of Upper Elementary Students' Reading, Writing, and Communication in Digital Spaces." *Reading Research Quarterly* 51 (4): 435–54.

Hwang, Gwo Jen, Po Han Wu, Ya Yen Zhuang, and Yueh Min Huang. 2013. "Effects of the Inquiry-Based Mobile Learning Model on the Cognitive Load and Learning Achievement of Students." *Interactive Learning Environments* 21 (4): 338–54.

International Literacy Association. 2018. "Improving Digital Practices for Literacy, Learning, and Justice." https://www.literacyworldwide.org/docs/default-source/where-we-stand/ila-improving-digital-practices-literacy-learning-justice.pdf.

Jeong, Se-Hoon, Hyuyi Cho, and Yoori Hwang. 2012. "Media Literacy Interventions: A Meta-Analytic Review." *Journal of Communication* 62: 454–72.

Kahne, Joseph, and Benjamin Bowyer. 2017. "Educating for Democracy in a Partisan Age: Confronting Challenges of Motivated Reasoning and Misinformation." *American Educational Research Journal* 54: 3–34.

Kyndt, Eva, Elisabeth Raes, Bart Lismont, Fran Timmers, Eduardo Cascallar, and Filip Dochy. 2013. "A Meta-Analysis of the Effectives of Face-to-Face Cooperative Learning: Do Recent Studies Falsify or Verify Earlier Findings?" *Educational Research Review* 10: 133–49.

Lakala, Minna, Jiri Lallimo, and Kai Hakkarainen. 2005. "Teachers' Pedagogical Designs for Technology-Supported Collective Inquiry: A National Case Study." *Computers & Education* 45 (3): 337–56.

Little, Callie W., Jacouri C. Clark, Tani E. Novell, and Carol McDonald Connor. 2018. "Improving Writing Skills Through Technology-Based Instruction: A Meta-Analysis." *Review of Education* 6 (2): 183–201.

MacArthur, Charles A. 2006. "The Effects of New Technologies on Writing and Writing Processes." In *Handbook of Writing*